Sunset

Tile
REMODELING HANDBOOK

A kitchen work area is transformed by a simple arrangement of floral tiles: with touches of lively color and lilting lines, imported glazed ceramic tiles create a delightfully cheerful corner. Design: Phyllis Brooks Interiors. Architect: The Bob Flury Group.

By the Editors
of Sunset Books and
Sunset Magazine

Sunset Publishing Corporation, Menlo Park, California

Tile: Colorful, decorative . . . and practical

When you're remodeling or decorating and it's time to consider surfacing materials, tile should be among your top choices—its qualities are hard to beat. Featured throughout this book are the three most common kinds of tile: ceramic, resilient, and wood.

Color photographs on the first 32 pages provide a sampling of ideas for the many uses of tile. The remainder of the book is a how-to-do-it guide—abundantly illustrated with drawings and diagrams—to help you choose, install, and care for the tile. Since there are so many kinds available commercially, always be sure to follow any specifications provided by the manufacturer of the tile you're using. This advice also applies to supplemental tiling materials, such as adhesives and grouts.

We would like to thank Faye Byrnes of Western Tile Distributors for her assistance in preparing the manuscript. Thanks also go to JoAnn Masaoka for scouting locations and styling some of the photographs in this book, and to Bob Smithers for his assistance in location scouting for the front cover.

Produced by The Compage Company, San Francisco
in cooperation with the Sunset Editors

Book Editor: Philip Cecchettini

Contributing Editor: Jeff Williams

Design: Joe di Chiarro

Illustrations: Rik Olson
Terrence Meagher

Photographers: Armstrong Cork Company: 28 top right.
Edward Bigelow: 6 right, 7, 8, 9 left, 10, 11 left, 13 top, 14, 15 bottom, 16, 18 right, 20, 21 left, 22 top, 23 top, 24, 26 top and left, 27 top left and bottom, 28 bottom, 30, 31 bottom. **Color Tile Supermart, Inc.:** 12 left, 21 right. **Steve Marley:** 1, 2, 3, 4–5, 9 right, 12 right, 13 left and right, 15 top, 17 top and bottom left, 18 left, 19 top and bottom left, 22 bottom, 23 bottom left and right, 25, 27 top right, 28 top left, 29 bottom left and right, 31 top, 32. **Jack McDowell:** 11 right, 26 bottom right. **Rob Super:** 29 top. **Tom Wyatt:** 6 left, 17 bottom right, 19 bottom right.

Cover: *You can spice up your kitchen by redecorating with tile. Attractive and easy to maintain, ceramic tile is perfect for areas that get a lot of use, like this work corner, lined with handpainted Portuguese squares and trim. Design: Esther H. Reilly, ASID. Cover design: Williams and Ziller Design. Photograph: Tom Wyatt.*

Large hexagonal Mexican pavers set up a bold pattern in this entry and living room, while the earth tone subdues the overall effect. Square pavers simplify tiling of the steps. Architect: Peter C. Rodi/Designbank.

Editor, Sunset Books: Elizabeth L. Hogan

Fourth printing May 1991

Contents

The luster of high-glaze ceramic tile and the unusual molded edging create a feeling of luxury in this bathroom. The 3¼" squares and matching rope detail are imported from Japan. Interior Decorator: Jane Starr. Architect: J. Allen Sayles, Architectural Kitchens and Baths.

Tile in Color
. . . ceramic, resilient, and wood

It's sort of magic, the way in which tile adapts itself so easily to every style and taste—you can match any mood, create any kind of appearance. Merely choose among the hundreds, even thousands of tile designs, textures, sizes, shapes, and colors available to evolve just the effect you've been imagining for your home.

And tile is not only for your floors and countertops. Try it on walls or even ceilings; trim doors and windows, fireplaces or mirrors; give your staircase a lift with decorated tile risers; add a special quality to the environment of your home with house numbers, supergraphics, or even tiles custom-designed just for you. To see what we mean, take a stroll through the following pages. You're sure to come away with a few ideas of your own.

The tremendous versatility of tile
is demonstrated here: the same tile that covers the dining area marches right out onto the patio—and lines countertops and walls as well. This handmade Mexican Saltillo tile is sealed for indoor use and left in its natural state for outdoors. It is inexpensive, widely available, and easy to install. Architect: Batey & Mack, Architects.

Commercial Tile: Tasteful and Inventive

Commercial tile might be considered commonplace, but one look at this collection of beautiful floors should counteract that impression. Though uniform in appearance and widely available, commercial tile applied tastefully and inventively in suitable surroundings almost guarantees impressive results.

Manufacturers often provide a single type of tile in a wide range of colors, allowing you to select a small group of colors for a graphic design or a monochromatic theme. Unusual shapes such as hexagons, octagons, or even floral motifs will add visual interest to your floors. Or you can achieve a special look by using tile *seconds*. Usually sold at a low price, seconds can be put to excellent use, for any defects are usually quirks in appearance rather than deformities in the tiles themselves.

Tile Seconds: Impressive but Economical

At least five different shades of blue in a random mix fuse visually to form this floor of 2" square ceramic tiles. Leftovers from larger orders and pieces with slight irregularities, these tiles were purchased as seconds at a little more than half the normal retail price. Architect: Thaddeus E. Kusmierski.

Square Root

A lively geometry is created by this juxtaposition of two tile patterns. White tiles (divided into quarters by crisp blue lines) mate perfectly with the staggered array of blue tiles (divided into sixteenths by white lines) marching resolutely to the tub. Imported from Italy, these glazed tiles measure 8" by 8". Architect: William B. Remick.

A Scattering of Blooms

Recurring costs for floor refinishing induced the owners of this older Mexican-style home to tile the whole main floor with shaped ceramic paver tiles. Extruded into flat sheets and cut with cookie-cutter-like tools, three shapes create an interlocking floral pattern when laid with thin-set over the flat surface of the existing wood floor. Occasional paste waxing adds shine, protects tile surface. Design: The Tile Shop, Berkeley, California.

Framing Your Tile

As an alternative to an all-wood or all-tile floor, 8" hexagonal ceramic tiles lie within prelaid strips of oak flooring, each material complementing the other. Placement of strips and tile requires careful planning. Architect: Churchill-Zlatunich Associates.

Quarry Tile Floors: Simple and Elegant

Quarry tile—large, uniform, and devoid of decoration—is the most likely way to floor an entire home in ceramic tile. Usually available in natural clay colors, quarry tiles range from a raw, earthy Mexican appearance to the smartly sophisticated look of French glazed tiles. The four examples given here show you the versatility of this material and the various forms in which it is available to you.

Most quarry tile is easy to maintain. For glazed types, damp-mopping is sufficient; unglazed quarry keeps its looks if treated with a sealer and then waxed periodically.

The Look of Leather, the Permanence of Tile
Used throughout the house, glazed 12" by 12" terra cotta quarry tile has a leatherlike appearance because of its rounded corners and edges and slightly uneven surface. Staggering the rows of tile adds visual interest. Architect: Fred Blecksmith.

Paver Tiles Add Punch
Distinguished by a rich brown patina from years of waxing and use, 6" by 10" machine-made clay paver tiles have an interesting surface of grooves and ridges formed as each tile was extruded. Architect: A. Quincy Jones.

Down to Earth

The idiosyncratic character of sunbaked Mexican quarry tile, with its natural variations in texture and color, will appeal to those who like a casual look. Large six-sided tiles, stained and sealed, contrast dramatically with white walls, and the glazed ceramic tiles on the kitchen walls pick up the floor color. Design: Dagmar Thiel, Kitchen and Bath Design.

Tiles for a Mexican Mood

Glazed 12" by 12" Mexican quarry tiles set with wide bands of white grout are effective as a flooring material throughout this Spanish-style home. Glazed quarry tiles are durable and easy to clean. Window trim of hand-decorated and glazed 4" by 4" Mexican tiles was set into the wall before plastering, so wall face is flush with tiles. Architect: Alfred T. Gilman. Design: Windom Hawkins.

Tile Floors for Entryways . . . A Warm Welcome

Home entryways really do have a special function: they say "welcome" to the outside world and give the visitor a glimpse of what awaits within. The tiled versions shown on these two pages have vastly different personalities, yet all invite the viewer to become further acquainted.

A decorative tile entry can be pared down to simple eloquence, as in the entry below, or expanded into a more complex overall pattern uniting indoors and out (see photo on page 11, lower right). The ruglike entry at left hints at an ethnic solution, while a field of black diamonds defines the entryway and divides the floor space of the home on page 11, left. Each solution is different, yet each is highly successful.

Ethnic Mix of Custom and Commercial Tiles
Hand-decorated, glazed tiles create patterns simulating ethnic rug designs of American Indian or African origin. Unglazed 4" by 6" tiles separating rows of repeat designs make this an economical decorating idea. Design: Linda Rowlands with Barbara Vantrease Beall Studio.

Glazed Tile Entry Strip
A wide band of 12" by 12" glazed quarry tile set three tiles deep is flush with exterior entry and interior floor, effectively dividing these areas. Architect: Buff and Hensman, Architects and Associates.

Diamonds Define the Entry
The mock slate texture of cast clay tile, combined with the effect of black tile insets in a field of octagonal tiles, sets this entry area apart from the rest of a fully tiled interior. The diagonal set of white tiles in the background adds subtle visual interest to an open expanse of floor. Architect: Peter Choate.

De la Casa al Patio
A truly versatile flooring, low-fired Mexican pavers are at home inside or on the patio. Pointed pickets add pattern variety. Indoors, pavers are coated with masonry sealer; outdoors, they're left bare. Architect: Edward Giddings.

Tile in the Kitchen

Here's a quintet of ideas for using tile in the kitchen. Below, countertop tile is repeated on the fireplace, helping to unite kitchen and adjoining family room. At left, glazed quarry tile and patterned resilient tile echo each other in a subtle harmony of earth tones.

The three photos opposite feature creative tile details: a durable *trompe l'oeil* rug, a tile border set in plaster, and a kitchen backsplash tiled with hardwood slices. Other kitchen ideas are shown on pages 14 and 15.

Dark Drama
This kitchen achieves an earthy elegance through a creative combination of ceramic and resilient tile. Rich brown glazed quarry tile is used on all work surfaces; on the floor, vinyl tile in similar but lighter tones adds subtle pattern interest. Color coordination is the key to the unified look. Design: Color Tile Supermart, Inc.

Cook's-eye View
From the vantage point of the counter workspace, lined with matte-glazed ceramic tile, the cook can enjoy the beauty of a blazing fire—and an attractive fireplace, adorned with matching tile. Architect: Moyer Associates.

A Permanent Persian
One way to avoid cleaning bills: design and install a hand-painted and glazed Persian rug. Or create your own area rug with decorated commercial tiles, then trim it with custom-painted and glazed fringe. Surrounding area is finished inexpensively with plain commercial tile. Design: Barbara Van-trease Beall Studio.

Old Tiles, New Statement
In this remodeled historic adobe home, handpainted Mexican tiles stand out cheerfully around an uncurtained window. Set directly in damp plaster, these tiles could also create the same effect if set and patched into chipped-out areas of existing plaster. Architect: Will Shaw.

Wood Tiles Work Wonders
Unique 4" by 4" Uruguayan hardwood end-grain tiles form intriguing backsplash display. Fastened directly to the wall without grout, in the sequence they were cut, these textural tiles complement the 3" cobalt blue ceramic tile countertop and its wooden edging. Design: Al Garvey.

A Handpainted Botanical Design

The wall area behind the cooktop is a natural for creative decor; this custom handpainted and glazed botanical design proves the point. The design relates both to the canisters at right and to a subtle but effective handpainted and glazed counter trim design. Design: Barbara Vantrease Beall Studio.

Rustic Repeats Give Counter the Edge

Another way to edge a counter: a 90° angle formed with 4" by 4" and 2" by 4" hand-decorated Mexican tiles. White ground unifies the surface, giving the limelight to the tile decoration itself. Architect: Alfred T. Gilman. Design: Windom Hawkins.

Tile Shelving

Kitchen shelf storage gets a pick-me-up with plain 4" by 4" white glazed commercial tiles. Easy to clean, these shelves are finished with sink cap tiles, a raised and rounded edging that keeps stored items from rolling off a shelf.
Design: Barbara Vantrease Beall Studio.

Kitchen Tile Highlights

You needn't spread tile throughout your kitchen to achieve a delightfully detailed look. A few tile designs judiciously selected and applied will give a real uplift to an otherwise simply functional work area.

Countertops and walls are the likeliest candidates for change, but to give your kitchen a real custom look, consider working with defined spaces such as the area behind the cooktop or the kickplates below the lower cabinets. If you're interested in ceramics, you might even design and make your own decorative tiles for a truly personalized kitchen.

A Country Accent
An assortment of charming rustic characters, informally arranged, emerge from a cream-colored background to enliven the splash behind this tiled counter. Imported from Japan, these tiles are handpainted in natural earth tones and glazed to a matte finish. Design: Gabriella Bowling.

Kickplate of Culinarios Tiles
Instead of a wood or metal kickplate, try trimming your kitchen floor with culinarios tiles instead. Though the tiles shown here were custom handpainted and glazed, other versions are readily available commercially. Design: Barbara Vantrease Beall Studio.

Creative Baths with Commercial Tile

Inventive yet tasteful, the ten tile installations on the following four pages all use commercial ceramic tile to complete the promise of a well-designed bath environment. Decorative touches in each bath design make use of inherent characteristics of tile; plant niches, curved surfaces, supergraphics, contrasting colors, and other design ideas give each bath a distinct personality based on the standard, repeatable appearance of commercial tiles.

Getting the Angle on a Great Graphic
Plain 4" by 4" commercial tiles can make strong graphic statements: cutting some tiles diagonally enabled the architect to build an expansive wraparound design for this soaking tub and shower enclosure. Architect: Gary Gilbar.

Clean-Cut European
Two colors of 1" square tessarae tile define both form and function in a modern Italian-style bath. Bright red floor grouted in white joins the main bath to an open shower in rear, optically expanding the appearance of what is essentially a standard-size bathroom. Tiles come in 12" by 12" mesh-back sheets. Architect: David Raphael Singer.

Shower in the Great Outdoors
A secluded, woodsy setting inspired the inclusion of the dramatic window in this sunken tub and shower. Simply elegant, these 3" by 6" green tiles, glazed to a glossy shine, are custom-set in a prepared mortar bed. Architects: Ellmore/Titus.

Blue Heaven
This uncompromisingly modern guest bath would look at home aboard a starship cruising some far-off galaxy in the distant future. But the imported tile is available today—right here on earth. An imaginative arrangement of closely related tile patterns creates this dazzling effect.
Architect: Weston Whitfield.

A Soaking Tub . . . Tile Inside and Out
Rather than outfitting this large area in expensive hand-decorated tile, a single design of handpainted Italian tile is used as trim for plain rectangular tiles, creating an Egyptian-style custom bath. Design: Ray and Jackie Rossi, Designed Environ, Inc.

The Shape of Elegance

The graceful curve of this bathtub is accentuated by the linear tile design on the side—and further underscored by the recessed lighting below. The broad waterfall spout adds an unusual touch, and the tile floor, patterned with individual diamonds and squares, carries out the color scheme. A luxurious effect—yet the tile is readily available and not expensive. Design: Dagmar Thiel, Kitchen and Bath Design.

Scenic Trim Goes Traditional

A large expanse of decoration isn't necessary to make a tile environment come alive. This tastefully restrained bath with shower features a narrow band of handpainted and glazed 4" by 6" tiles in a running hunt scene. Decorated outer base trim banding and diagonally set shower floor unify the decor, which is completed with plain 4" by 6" commercial tiles. Design: Barbara Vantrease Beall Studio.

A Sculptured Environment

Plaster, wood, glass, and tile create an expansive custom-built bath environment. The sunken tile tub takes advantage of a city view, while three-dimensional, amorphous plaster walls finish off previously laid tile areas above the countertop. Architect: Igor Sazevich.

Plants Find Their Niche

Modern in mood, this step-in tile shower of 12" by 12" glazed quarry tiles has built-in 6" by 11" square plant niches of the same tile to take advantage of the skylight and the moist environment. Architect: Buff and Hensman, Architects and Associates.

Step Up to Relaxation

The neutral tones of off-white tile and unstained knotty pine provide the perfect backdrop for striking accents and borders of hand-decorated Mexican ceramic tile. A shower, seen through an etched glass window, is framed and lined with tile to match. Design: Diane Johnson Design.

The Total Tile Bath

Bathrooms have a special place in the hearts of many who consider water as one of the elemental joys of life. These connoisseurs find nothing too good for the space in which they perform their daily toilette. Witness the four unique offerings served up on these two pages.

These imaginative baths give esthetic answers to practical questions. The tiles range from costly custom patterns to handsome yet budget-minded products available coast-to-coast. In each case, though, their function is the same: to provide durable beauty in a room that too often is only utilitarian.

A Charming Chameleon
A process called fuming produced the unusual iridescent quality of these 11" by 11" glazed Italian tiles. The appearance of the tile alters from pink to gold to blue as light passes across the tub enclosure. French glass 1" hexagons on mesh backing form the curved backrest and floor of the tub. Design: Tom McGraw with International Tile and Supply Corporation.

The Greenhouse Goes Indoors
A bath environment of ferns and vines integrates tub enclosure and shelf/seating area. Handpainted and glazed 6" by 6" tiles were first numbered on backs according to a graphed layout plan, then installed over a waterproofed lath-and-cement tub surround. Design: Barbara Vantrease Beall Studio.

Beauty through Simplicity

Two widely available commercial tile patterns combine in this adaptable bathroom design. One pattern is used on the walls, the other primarily on the floor. An accent band of the floor tile adds a dramatic touch to the walls. Design: Color Tile Supermart, Inc.

Shower Ahoy!

The impressive hand-decorated and glazed tiles of this shower wall form the focal point of a nautically decorated boy's bath. Though tiling a shower enclosure may require a pro, the effect obtained can be extraordinary. Note the diagonal pattern of plain tiles on the shower floor. Design: Barbara Vantrease Beall Studio.

Tile Finishes around Sinks

Sometimes the little details are what make a tile job stand out. These five examples show how the inherent qualities of a tile type can be enhanced by special finishing treatments.

You needn't settle for a conventional method of installing or completing a tile job. In fact, the more creative you are in dealing with a common situation, the more personalized your finished installation will appear. Though two of the methods shown here—the quarter-round and the mitered edging—are jobs for experienced tile setters if not professionals, the other methods are within reach of most do-it-yourselfers.

Wet Bar—Simple but Effective

A built-in wet bar gets a dramatic lift with the application of chocolate-colored, scraffito-decorated 6" by 6" Mexican tiles. This would be easy for the homeowner who wants a weekend job with maximum impact. Note wooden counter edge. Architect: Bernard Judge.

From the Potter's Hand

This custom-made basin and matching tile display the individuality and fine craftsmanship that may be achieved when an object is lovingly handmade by one person. Two ducks soar in a sky of blue porcelain, surrounded by shades of luminous blue tile, which show faint impressions of the canvas upon which the tiles were rolled. Architect: William Zimmerman.

South of the Border Style

The bold vine pattern of this bathroom basin is repeated in the surrounding trim of hand-decorated and glazed Mexican tiles. Bullnose tile pieces, traditionally used for edgings, create an attractive trim for the backsplash, while 4" by 4" and 2" by 4" tiles edge the countertop itself.
Architect: Alfred T. Gilman. Design: Windom Hawkins.

Quarter-Round Trim Treatment

Narrow quarter-round tile pieces set in a mortar base offer an attractive alternative for bathroom basin trim. Cutting tiles to fit and floating them into mortar are both difficult and time-consuming tasks. Design: Tile by Buzz.

Bevel-Edged Beauty

Standard tile trims don't always come in colors or sizes you need. An interesting solution: this custom bevel-edged counter uses 1" tiles set at angles in a mortar base for a stunning trim.
Architect: Wayne Wedell.

Tile Complements the Hearth

At the heart of many homes is the fireplace. Originally intended as functional heating devices, fireplaces have developed over the years into decorative focal points as well. Here are four different versions using tile—each with its own brand of function and style.

Tile is an ideal material for fireplace use as an alternative to the usual brick, cement, or metal enclosure. Impervious to heat and easy to clean because of its glossy surface, ceramic tile also provides a medium for artistic expression. Though custom-designed tiles have been used in three of the four installations shown here, well-designed commercial tiles could do the job with equal success.

Flame Amid Flowers
Custom-painted and glazed, these 6" by 6" tiles with garland pattern give this fireplace a light and open aspect. This installation is a good weekend project for the conscientious do-it-yourselfer. Design: Barbara Vantrease Beall Studio.

California-Style Floral Fireplace
These custom-designed handpainted and glazed tiles feature bright flowers bordered by bands of yellow. After the 6" by 6" tiles were set around the face of the fireplace, plaster of the surrounding wall was gradually built up flush with the tile. Design: Barbara Vantrease Beall Studio.

A Garland Frame

Lush with magnolia blossoms, these custom-made hand-decorated and glazed tiles join with a handsome wood mantel to update an old brick fireplace. Installation was fairly simple: tiles were applied to existing bricks with mastic. Had brick surface been uneven, however, a mortar base would have been necessary. Design: Susan Tait, The Tile Shop, Berkeley, California.

A Classic Simplicity

Framing this old-fashioned fireplace with a single row of French-blue tile reinforces its simple and dignified lines. But the scroll-like design of these handpainted Portuguese tiles introduces richness and complexity. The quarry hearth tiles have been stained to blend with the wood of the floor, then sealed. Architect: J. Allen Sayles, Architectural Kitchens and Baths.

Effective Tile Accents

Here's a collection of inventive tile applications that use everything from commercial tiles to one-of-a-kind handmade and hand-decorated tiles. Often only a small amount of tile is required for an attractive and functional project, but sometimes a truly impressive effect can be achieved through use of a large expanse of tile in an unusual location, such as the ceiling on page 27.

Most of these installations are ones you could take on yourself; some could be accomplished in a weekend. If you choose a project like the buffet pictured at right, you may need a few additional skills, such as a knowledge of carpentry.

Serviceable Sideboard
Antique wall brackets support this simple but striking dining room buffet. Although rectangular 2" by 8" tiles set in herringbone fashion require some cutting for proper fit, installation is relatively easy and inexpensive.

Water Sprite
A musical maiden sits among lily pads in this all-tile shower. The tile picture "hangs" just above a built-in seat, where it helps to decorate not only the shower but also the rest of the bathroom—a large space that includes the fireplace at left. Architect: Glen William Jarvis.

Tile Risers Brighten Stairs
Work wonders in a weekend with just a few well-placed tiles. These stair risers, though decorated with custom-painted and glazed 4" by 6" tiles, could as easily be done with commercially available designs. Design: Barbara Vantrease Beall Studio.

Dancing on the Ceiling

Ceiling panels of custom-painted and glazed 6" by 6" tiles enliven an interior of dark wood and white walls. The tiles in each panel were anchored in thin-set adhesive row by row from a ladder-and-plank platform. Architect: Edward Carson Beall. Design: Barbara Vantrease Beall Studio.

Feline Fancy

For a custom look at an affordable price, a world of commercial accent tiles awaits the inventive decorator. Here the starkness of a white bathroom is interrupted by a surprising dash of color, as a queenly cat presides in a row of glossy black tile. Three more accent tiles, each picturing a different cat, complete this child's bathroom decor.
Architect: William B. Remick.

Custom Stoneware

Cut, painted, and glazed by hand, these unusual 4" by 6" stoneware tiles were created by the artist specifically for this bathroom installation. The subdued earth tones of the glaze are reinforced by the use of stone gray grout.
Architect: Bernard Judge. Design: Dora de Larios.

Design on the Diagonal
Embossed resilient tiles positioned on the diagonal add a strong regional flair to this cozy den accented with American Indian motifs. By avoiding conventional installation, the designer not only emphasized the strength of the tile design but also visually enlarged a basically small room. Design: Armstrong Cork Company.

Smooth as Slate
The classic mood of this bed-sitting room owes much to a carefully selected floor covering of white, slate-textured resilient tiles. Offsetting the squares in a checkerboard arrangement develops interesting patterns of light and shadow on this flooring.

Brick on a Budget
A strong offset brick pattern of resilient tiles blends with hand-painted and glazed culinarios ceramic tiles on countertop and splash. The result: a cheerful kitchen with a country look. Easy on the feet and the back, resilient tile is a good choice for kitchen work areas. Kitchen Design: Diane Johnson. Countertop Tile Design: Barbara Vantrease Beall Studio.

Wood and Resilient Tiles . . . Attractive Alternatives

Resilient and parquet tiles are two extremely versatile alternatives to ceramic tile. As with ceramics, both come in standard sizes and shapes that are easy to apply. The examples here merely give a sampling of the many patterns available in each type of product.

Resilient tiles can pretend to any number of personalities, from brick to slate or even ceramic. Parquet, on the other hand, has a distinct identity of its own. An aura of permanence and well-bred style surrounds this wood product, for it adds a feeling of old-world quality to practically any environment.

Patterns in Gold
Oak parquet tiles in the traditional Mount Vernon pattern yield warmth and richness in this breakfast room floor. Each tile is composed of five strips contained in a mitered frame of the same strips. Put together, the tiles give the effect of squares surrounded by pointed pickets. Architect: Peter W. Behn.

The Warmth of Wood
This unusual oak parquet kitchen counter consists of 6" square tiles set perpendicular to one another in mastic, then framed in oak trim and varnished for protection. Each tile consists of seven ⁷⁄₈" by 6" solid strips of wood held together by metal splines. Design: Charles Bliss.

Being Expansive with Parquet
Placing fingered parquet tiles in parallel rows, rather than in a checkerboard pattern as in the photograph at left, creates an entirely different feeling that visually expands this living area. Architect: John Brooks Boyd.

Taking Tile Out-of-Doors

Though tiles appear predominantly in interior settings on the previous pages, don't forget that their attractive permanence makes them ideal for outdoor use as well. These four interesting ideas add a level of quality and taste to otherwise mundane, functional situations.

Murals and trims are simple additions to exterior environments; these installations are well within the scope of a weekend do-it-yourself project. The mailboxes and entry steps require more planning and construction time—but the results would enhance the exterior of any home.

Letter-Perfect Mailboxes
A neighborhood project for experienced do-it-yourselfers: mailboxes with a custom handpainted and glazed ceramic plaque for each box. The stone and concrete structure was built around the boxes, which were then faced with plaques and wood trim. Design: Barbara Vantrease Beall Studio.

Tile Plaques in the Mayan Manner
Limited front yard space spurred owners to substitute this decorative wood and tile wall for established plantings. The hand-decorated and glazed 6" by 6" tiles were first mounted without grout on wood panels, then set into the fence. Design: Joan Fey with Barbara Vantrease Beall Studio.

Tiles over Concrete

Sand-colored tiles, patterned after the floor Jefferson created for Monticello, transform cold concrete slabs into a more congenial entry. The existing slab is decorated by individual hexagon and square tiles laid on a mastic base to form a large overall octagonal pattern. You can complete each block individually before moving on to the next one. Design: Ray and Jackie Rossi, Designed Environ, Inc.

Tile Trim's Warm Welcome

Handpainted and glazed 4″ by 4″ tiles with circular motifs edge a wood-trimmed entryway. The wall was prepared by attaching a 2″ by 4″ wooden backing along the edge of the door: tiles were then applied to the backing with thin-set adhesive. A 2″ wide metal strip conceals the raw edges of wood and tile. Design: Barbara Vantrease Beall Studio.

Ceramic Tile
. . . a colorful, lasting surface

Molded plastic spacers *help the tile setter to lay correctly and space glazed quarry tiles in mastic on a plywood subfloor. The spacers should be pried up and removed when mastic sets.*

Whether you are building a new home or remodeling an older one, you'll find few surfacing materials that match the decorative impact, versatility, and permanence of ceramic tile.

Basically just flat pieces of hard-baked clay, ceramic tiles provide a surface that's fireproof, durable, soil and moisture-resistant, and easy to maintain. A tiled surface is a group of tiles, each fastened with an adhesive (also known as a bonding agent or a bond coat) to a subsurface, or backing, and usually bonded to its neighbors with a filler material called grout.

Ceramic tile comes in a seemingly endless variety of colors, patterns, and textures. In addition to the pleasure tile will give you, its beauty and durability will add value to your home.

When you use ceramic tile, you are using a proven product. It is one of the oldest, most successful surfacing materials: tiles have been found in ancient Egyptian and Roman homes and baths. Brilliantly colored ceramic tiles still beautify the floors, walls, and ceilings of cathedrals, temples, and palaces built many centuries ago.

Where to Use Ceramic Tile

At one time, the use of ceramic tile in the home was restricted to bathrooms and an occasional foyer. Around the turn of the century, however, ceramic tile became popular for almost any room in the house. Today, ceramic tile is found on floors, walls, storage shelves, kitchen counters, and backsplashes; as table tops or decorative insets; around tubs and showers; and even on ceilings. Some ceramic tiles are even suitable for garden and patio paving.

Floors. Ceramic tile is a natural for floors. Nothing tolerates foot traffic as well as tile. In entryways, halls, and other heavy-traffic corridors, ceramic floor tiles remain rigid and colorfast. An onslaught of wet galoshes or the innocent tracking of a muddy family pet will do no harm to the floor. In the kitchen or bathroom, ceramic tile provides excellent protection against drips and spills; cleaning requires only a damp sponge or cloth.

Tiled flooring adds a strong decorative accent. Depending on the tile, you can create any atmosphere from elegance to rustic informality. Brighten a dark room with a tile floor or make a room look larger by extending the tile floor onto the patio or deck.

Walls. Any wall that might be sprayed or splashed with water is an obvious candidate for ceramic tile. Around bathtubs and showers, tile provides a waterproof surface that is easy to keep clean of water spots and soap film. But don't limit tile to areas that get wet. A wall of ceramic tile in a living room, dining room, or den adds a dramatic backdrop for furnishings, plants, or a free-standing fireplace.

Countertops. Ideal as a working surface around the kitchen sink and stove top, ceramic tile is equally unaffected by a sharp knife edge or a hot pan. Grease and food spots wipe off easily. Tile also adds a functional, decorative surface to a bathroom vanity, an eating counter, or a wet bar. Adding a new ceramic tile top will give new life to an old table; tile also adds flair to exposed storage shelves.

Fireplaces. Because they are baked at high temperatures, better-quality ceramic tiles are not affected by heat. Consider using tiles to line the inner edge or outside face of a fireplace. Even a single row will brighten a room.

Stairs and steps. Constant traffic wears down the treads of stairs and steps. Covering them with tiles will add years of life. For indoor or outdoor steps, use tiles with a slip-resistant textured finish. And for a simple brightening effect, tile the risers to make the steps more distinctive and visible in dim light.

Decorative borders. Set edge-to-edge or spaced apart, tiles make a beautiful accent border for a door or window. If fastened to the surface and left raised, they may require a wood or metal border trim. In new construction it is relatively simple to set border or trim tiles right into the plaster or stucco so the tile faces are flush with the finished wall.

Outdoors. Many kinds of ceramic tiles are suitable for outdoor use as a paving material or decorative surfacing. Extending the tile floor of a room outside to a patio creates a strong visual tie, making both areas appear larger. A garden pool rimmed with colorful tile or a tiled fountain and reflecting pool can highlight your yard.

About Ceramic Tile

Once you have decided to use ceramic tile, you have a wide array of choices. Tiles may be glazed or unglazed. You'll see pavers, patio tiles, quarry tiles, and ceramic mosaics. There are wall tiles, floor tiles, and counter tiles. Once you understand the basics, you can base your tiling plans on the different types, characteristics, colors, and uses.

Tile bodies are rated according to how easily they absorb water. Porcelain is the most vitreous (glasslike), most water-resistant tile. The best porcelain is highly refined clay fired at more than 2,000 ° to fuse the clay particles into a dense, hard body. Nonvitreous, or soft-bodied, tiles readily absorb water; treatment with a sealant makes them water-resistant only to a degree.

Glazed Tile

Glaze is a hard finish, usually including a color, applied to the surface of the clay body (the bisque) before final baking. Glazes can have a high gloss, a satin-like matte, a semimatte, or a dull, pebbly textured surface.

Unglazed Tile

Unglazed tiles do not have a baked-on surface. The colors you see, commonly earth tones ranging from yellow to dark red, are either the natural clay color or pigments added prior to forming and baking. This color is not applied and is consistent throughout the body of the tile.

Finishes *on ceramic tiles vary from dull unglazed surfaces to shiny glazed ones. Shown here from bottom to top: unglazed, matte, semi-matte, and bright glossy finish.*

Different Tile Types

There are four basic classifications of ceramic tiles according to their use: floor tiles, wall tiles, counter tiles, and ceramic mosaics.

Floor Tiles

Available glazed or unglazed, floor tiles are generally larger, thicker, and harder than wall tiles. Their superior strength makes them durable underfoot. Floor tiles come as squares, rectangles, hexagons, and octagons as well as in Moorish, ogee, and other exotic shapes (see next page).

Unglazed tile has advantages for floor use. It is less slippery, and wear does not show because the coloration extends throughout the body. Some glazed floor tiles have textured or matte surfaces, which give better traction and longer wear.

There are four types of floor tiles: quarry tiles, pavers, patio tiles, and glazed tiles. (For installation pointers, see page 46).

Quarry tiles. These tiles are made by squeezing clay into forms under great pressure (an extrusion process) and then firing until quite hard. They come glazed or unglazed in natural clay colors of yellow, brown, or red. Tough and water-resistant (especially when sealed), quarry tile is an ideal flooring surface both indoors and out. Sizes and shapes vary, including $3\frac{7}{8}$″ by $3\frac{7}{8}$″, 6″ by $12\frac{3}{8}$″, or 8″ by 8″.

Pavers. Quite similar to quarry tiles, pavers are molded rather than extruded before they are fired. Pavers are generally unglazed and should be sealed to make them water-resistant. These rugged tiles are also available in many colors and sizes.

Patio tiles. Designed for outdoor use, patio tiles are softer and less regular in shape than quarry tiles or pavers. Made from natural clays—and often hand-made—they come in shades of red, tan, yellow and brown. Up to 1″ in thickness and 12″ by 12″ in size, patio tiles often have a rough appearance.

Because they absorb water easily, they may crack if frozen. If you live in an area with regular and severe winter freezes, ask your dealer about the best tile to use. Patio tiles will survive mild freezing, but the harder quarry or paver tiles are better for use in severe winter areas.

Glazed tiles. There are glazed tiles for floors and walls, but wall tiles are often softer and not suitable for floor use. For floor tiles, select a glaze that will not be dangerously slippery.

Button back tiles, often imported from Italy, have a series of small bumps on the underside that allow the tiles to be stacked in the kilns and still have air space between. These may crack if not bedded properly.

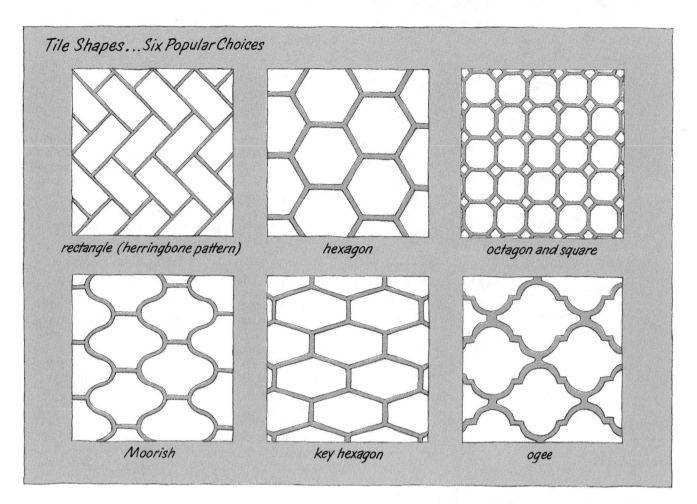

Tile Shapes...Six Popular Choices

rectangle (herringbone pattern)

hexagon

octagon and square

Moorish

key hexagon

ogee

Wall Tiles

Tiles classified as wall tiles are glazed and offer a great variety of colors and designs. Generally lighter and thinner than floor tiles, wall tiles are appropriate for use on walls and ceilings, both indoors and outdoors. They are fairly light—a plus for vertical installation. And though their bodies are porous, the glazing process makes their surface water-resistant. Wall tiles can be used on interior floors if traffic is light.

Standard sizes for wall tiles range from 3″ by 3″ to 4¼″ by 8½″, with thicknesses from ¼″ to ⅜″. As a visit to a dealer will show you, other sizes and shapes are available.

Many tiles come with matching trim pieces. Carrying such intriguing names as bullnose cap, eagle beak, and up butterfly, these specially shaped pieces are designed to finish off edges, form coves, and turn inside and outside corners (see illustrations at right). Some tiles have matching glazed ceramic accessories—soap dishes, towel bars, and glass and brush holders.

Wall tiles are now available in the form of pregrouted panels. Designed primarily for shower and tub areas, the panels contain up to sixty-four 4¼″ by 4¼″ tiles each. The savings in installation time are considerable. The panels are grouted with flexible, water-repellent silicone, urethane, or polyvinyl chloride rubber.

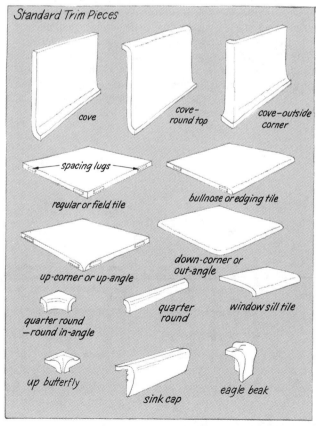

Standard Trim Pieces

cove

cove—round top

cove—outside corner

spacing lugs

regular or field tile

bullnose or edging tile

up-corner or up-angle

down-corner or out-angle

quarter round —round in-angle

quarter round

window sill tile

up butterfly

sink cap

eagle beak

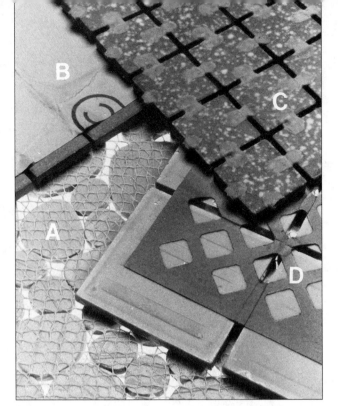

Mosaic tiles *come mounted on thread mesh (A), paper sheet (B), silicone rubber (C), and paper mesh (D). You may find tiles up to 6" square mounted in sheets.*

Counter Tiles

Counter tiles, as the name implies, are for covering kitchen and bath countertops. But they can be used on shelves, window sills, and table tops, or as decorative inserts in tables—whatever your imagination allows.

Counter tiles come in a wide variety of shapes, sizes, and colors, from basic whites to glowing reds or deep blues. Counter tiles are glazed, with a semi-gloss or high-gloss finish that makes wiping up spills easy.

A variety of special trim tiles allow you to tile around sinks, along counter edges, and around corners, or to put in a tile backsplash.

Ceramic Mosaics

Whether for floors or walls, mosaics are generally small: ¾" by ¾" on up to 4" by 4". Smaller tiles are mounted on plastic netting or joined together so you can lay out 1 or 2 square feet at a time. The shapes include squares, octagons, hexagons, or special designs.

Ceramic mosaics are among the most colorful and versatile materials in the tile family. They are striking on floors and walls, and the smaller ones can wrap around columns or follow the contours of garden walls and swimming pools.

Mosaics can be of natural clay tile or hard porcelain, and come both glazed and unglazed. Some mosaics contain a nonslip additive for safety.

Decorated Tiles

Handpainted tiles, often created for tile shops by artists in your locale, offer decorative flowers, trees, and animals. They can be set as individual accents in a backsplash, wall, or counter. Entire scenarios, such as a basket of flowers or swimming whales, can be painted on a group of tiles. Most handpainted tiles are done by professionals, but you can paint your own tiles and have them glazed.

Decals, cheaper than the handpainted tiles, but also attractive, can be applied to tiles. Your dealer can show you decals—again usually flowers or animals—that are permanently applied to the tiles through a firing process done in the store.

Choosing the Right Tile

Installing ceramic tile can be a sizable financial commitment. The permanence of tile is not compatible with a whimsical change of mind. Choosing a tile that meets both functional and decorative needs requires careful thought. Take time to shop around.

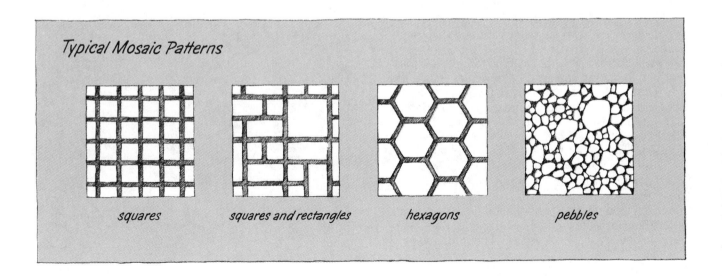

Typical Mosaic Patterns

squares   squares and rectangles   hexagons   pebbles

Consider Use First

How you will use the tile surface and where it will be installed are the two most important considerations. Will the surface be primarily decorative or must it stand up under a steady stream of traffic? Do you want to brighten a dark room or add a subdued rustic mood to a light study? If the family bathroom is the site, you'll have different requirements than you would for the entry hall. You have a lot to think about when considering your use of the tile, and you may want some help. Here are three ready sources of information.

Showrooms. Ceramic tile manufacturers, distributors, and dealers, as well as some licensed contractors, have showrooms displaying a great variety of tiles. Not only can you examine the tile, but you can see how it can be used in a sampling of actual situations—especially bathroom and kitchen settings. The showroom staff can answer your questions and advise you on tile selections, amounts, and costs. You can usually check out samples to try out at home for color, size, and compatibility.

(Continued on next page)

Seeing colors *and patterns of tiles in a showroom can help you make a choice.*

Tips on Designing with Tile

At one time or another, we've all been fooled by optical illusions— remember "Which is longer?" and "Which square is larger?" You can put these same illusions to work for you when you use tile colors, patterns, and designs to alter or control the apparent space in a room. Here are a few tips:

A busy tile pattern or a mix of several colors makes an area look smaller; using a simple pattern or a single color has the opposite effect.

Small tiles seem to expand the size of the tiled surface. Large tiles decrease the apparent size of the area.

Dark colors tend to shrink a given space . . .

. . . while light or bright colors impart an airy, spacious feeling.

To achieve visual unity, continue the same flooring from one room to the next or out onto an exterior patio area.

Divide space within a room into specific activity areas by using contrasting tile colors or patterns on the floor.

Put tile to work: *Repeated tile pattern running lengthwise adds depth to room; running across, it gives a shorter, wider look. Tile continued outside increases apparent space, adds visual unity.*

. . . Continued from page 37

Showrooms and the literature they offer can be important sources for ideas on types, colors, and possible patterns. In case you decide not to do the job yourself, most tile dealers have their own installers available.

Decorators and architects. These professionals specialize in combining esthetics and function. They can help you analyze your needs and find solutions to tricky decorating problems.

Tile contractors. Tile contractors may show you tile samples and advise you on some basic choices, but you should have your selection already in mind from your own legwork. You should get a written estimate of labor costs and of the tile costs if the contractor is purchasing it. The contractor can also advise you on potential structural problems, such as whether your subfloor will support a heavy tile floor.

The experienced hand of a licensed tile contractor is best for some projects. For example, installing swimming pool tile is not usually do-it-yourself work. Applications that require setting tiles in a full mortar bed, such as around a free-form or sunken tub, are best handled by a pro. Tile dealers and distributors can arrange a contractor for you, but if possible have one recommended by a satisfied customer.

Think about the Foundation

Tile, like a house, is only as strong as its foundation. The backing—the surface over which the ceramic tiles will be installed—is an important consideration when you choose tile. The composition and structural soundness of this surface not only limit the kinds of tile you can lay over it, but also determine the quality and durability of the finished tile surface. It is important to note that the surface must be quite smooth. If it is not, you will have to fix it or replace the backing (see page 44). Several common surfaces can be covered with tile, including new or existing wood, concrete, gypsum wallboard, and ceramic or resilient tile backings. These are discussed in the section on backings, beginning on page 43.

When in doubt . . . get advice. If you are unsure about the soundness of the surface to be tiled, consult a professional. Your tile dealer is the best free source. If you don't get satisfactory answers from the person in the showroom, make arrangements to talk directly with an installer. You can also pay a contractor to give you advice.

Consider Custom Tile & Glazing

If catalog searching and showroom shopping has left you without a satisfactory tile, consider having tile made to order. Customizing tile is done mostly in the glazing process. Custom tile manufacturers will glaze "raw" (unglazed) tiles to the color and pattern of your choice. You can also paint your own tiles and have them glazed. As a less expensive alternative, customize tile with decals.

Handpainted custom glazing can create almost any pattern you can imagine. A group of tiles can be deco-

rated to look like an exotic rug permanently glazed into the floor surface; a tiny corner piece can be accented with a delicate flower.

There are special tile manufacturers who create tile in odd shapes and sizes to fill specific custom design needs.

Buying Tile

Tile can cost from about $1 per square foot to nearly $40. Generally, the more tiles of a particular size, surface pattern, and glaze that are manufactured, the less each one will cost—a result of the efficiency of mass production. Special surface treatment, such as glazing and texturing, and manufacturing in smaller batches mean higher prices.

Single-color, glazed, flat-surfaced tiles—those commonly used around showers and tubs—are the most economical, sometimes less than $1 per square foot. The trim pieces for these tiles normally cost more per square foot than the regular tiles. Some patio tiles are also inexpensive. The addition of three-dimensional patterns and multicolored glazes can easily double costs. Other cost factors include the purity and density of the clay used and the temperature at which the tiles are baked. Purer clays fired at higher temperatures generally make costlier but better-wearing tiles.

Before You Buy

When you are ready to select and purchase your ceramic tile, follow these helpful tips.

Measure. Have accurate measurements ready for the area to be covered. A plan on graph paper helps you to visualize the area and provides a clue to the trim pieces you may need. Your tile dealer will help you figure out how many tiles you require.

Plan ahead. Some showrooms have only displays; others have catalogs featuring additional tile varieties. Be sure to plan enough time if you are ordering your tile.

Buy extra. Always buy more tiles that you need—the rule of thumb is to add 5 percent. This allows for the ones that are cut to the wrong size or that break while cutting. If a tile breaks or chips after installation, you'll have an extra to replace it. If you wait until damage occurs to buy replacement tiles, you may not be able to find pieces that match.

Check for color. Before you bring the tiles home, check the cartons to be sure the shades of color in the tile match. Different cartons of the same tile can vary significantly.

Watch for closeouts. A dealer will often sell closeouts at a discount. These may be tiles the manufacturer has discontinued, a color or pattern that was overstocked, or a supply of tiles left over from a large installation or a cancelled order.

Check the "bone pile." Another way to save money is to select tile from the dealer's or manufacturer's bone pile. These tiles, called seconds, are flawed or blemished (usually only slightly), so they cannot be sold with the regular stock at full price. Often these tiles will go undetected if randomly mixed with unblemished tile. However, watch out for seconds that have a pitted surface. When grout is spread, it may settle in these tiny holes and give the tiles a mottled effect.

Selecting Adhesive & Grout

When you buy ceramic tile, you should also get the materials for setting the tiles. Setting tile in a bed of mortar gives the most durable results, but it's a difficult job best left to a professional. Today, many professionals and amateurs alike are getting excellent results using adhesive to hold the tile to the backing and grout, a mortarlike material, to fill the joints between the tiles.

Several types of adhesives and grout are available, as described below. Your dealer can help you choose the products that are recommended for your tile, backing, and location.

Adhesives: Making It Stick

There are several types of tile adhesives, and they fall under three major categories: organic, commonly called mastics; cement-base, known as thin-sets; and epoxies, which are chemically activated resins. Make sure you choose an appropriate one for your situation.

For instructions on applying adhesives, see page 46.

Organic adhesives (mastics). Classified as organic because the adhesive was originally made from rubber-tree extracts, mastics are the most popular with do-it-yourselfers. Essentially a glue, they come pre-mixed in a thick liquid form. Solvent-base mastics, which have a strong odor, have largely been replaced by mastics with a latex base. The latex helps the mastics spread more easily and makes them water resistant; however, they are not absolutely waterproof. Top-quality mastics are excellent for normal floors and walls that will not be subjected to moisture.

Suitable backings for mastics include smooth plaster, gypsum wallboard, or plywood. Avoid using them when tiling over masonry.

Cement-base adhesives (thin-sets). Known in the trade as thin-sets because only a thin layer is used, these waterproof adhesives are made from premixed dry cement, sometimes with fine sand added. Unsanded thin-set is used where the grout joints are very narrow, as in mosaics; larger grout joints call for sand, which adds body to the thin-set mix.

Be sure to mix the adhesive according to the directions. The consistency should be stiff enough that the mortar ridges formed on the backing by a notched trowel

Adhesives and grouts come in bewildering variety; consult your dealer for proper selection.

do not slump or flow. A latex additive, called an admix, is commonly mixed with the dry material instead of water. The admix makes the adhesive easier to spread, reduces shrinkage, and increases the bonding quality.

Suitable backings for cement-base adhesives include dry cement slabs if completely free from paint and other coatings (see page 44), cement backer board, exterior grade plywood, gypsum wallboard, ceramic tile, marble, and brick. This type of adhesive isn't suitable for solid lumber surfaces, which are often too irregular and may swell when damp with the liquid in the mix. Cement-base adhesives don't adhere well to vinyl, asphalt, or linoleum surfaces.

Epoxy-base adhesives. A powerful and completely waterproof adhesive, epoxy is a top choice where water might be a problem, as in bathrooms and on countertops. It can also be used to fill irregular areas or low spots in flooring.

To make epoxy, you need to mix three ingredients: a resin, a hardening agent, and a dry mixture of cement and fine sand to give it more body. The new epoxies are easy to spread and to clean up; however, epoxy must be applied in a fairly narrow temperature range. Epoxy can cause skin and eye irritations, so work in a well-ventilated area and wear protective clothing.

Suitable backings for epoxy include dry concrete slabs (including those with radiant heat), backer board, gypsum wallboard, linoleum or resilient tile, ceramic tile, marble, and brick. It's the preferred adhesive for plywood backings.

Grouts: Attractive & Functional

Grout highlights the tile pattern and fills the joints between tiles, keeping out foreign matter such as dirt, food, and—if sealed—liquids. Because water and other liquids penetrating behind the tiles can discolor them and destroy the adhesive bond and backing, it's important to apply the grout correctly and to protect and care for it properly.

Whether you choose cement-base or epoxy grout, or silicone caulk as your grout depends on the tile you're using, its location, the width of the joint, and the adhesive. Also note that grout comes in many colors. It can be purchased precolored, or you can make up your own color. One caution with dark grout: if you're using unglazed tiles, seal them first, then test the grout with your tiles to make sure the grout doesn't stain them.

Instructions for applying and caring for grout are on pages 62–64.

Cement-base grouts. These grouts, widely used by both amateurs and professionals, come in packages that include Portland cement, which may or may not have sand added to it. Grout for mosaic tiles, for example, is unsanded. Though these grouts can be mixed with water, they're often mixed with a latex additive instead; the latex makes them easier to spread, increases the bond, and reduces shrinkage (which causes grout to crack). It also eliminates the need to cure the grout.

Similar to thin-set adhesive, these grouts are made more liquid to flow into the spaces between the tiles (and under them, if necessary) to fill any gaps in the adhesive. Though water resistant, they're not absolutely waterproof; you'll need to seal the grout after it has dried for a few days. Cement-base grouts can be used indoors or outdoors.

If you are putting down a large patio outside, you can mix your own grout on the job from sand, Portland cement, and water. It's virtually the same as a mortar mixed for setting tile or brick—just a little thinner. The ratio of cement to sand depends on the width of the joints between the tiles (see chart below). Add water slowly as you mix the ingredients; the final mix should be soft enough to be easily troweled into the joints, but not soupy.

Joint width	Cement	Sand
Less than 1/8″	1 part	0 part
1/8″ to 1/2″	1 part	2 parts
More than 1/2″	1 part	3 parts

Epoxy grouts. Because epoxy is waterproof, it's the grout of choice for any areas subject to moisture, such as bathrooms, sink counters, laundry rooms, and entry-

ways. It's also highly resistant to most chemicals, making it a good choice in a darkroom or workroom. You can use epoxy grouts with any tile adhesive, but they are more expensive than other grouts and slightly more difficult to work with.

Silicone rubber caulk. Commonly known as bathtub caulk, silicone rubber caulk stays permanently flexible, withstands extremes of cold and heat, repels water, and resists mildew. Generally, it's used as a grout only in pregrouted panels in showers or around shower-tub combinations. It comes in tubes or cartridges and is squeezed into the joints, not spread over the tile as grout is.

Silicone rubber caulk is most useful where surfaces tend to move slightly, such as where a wall meets a floor or where tiles abut wood trim. It's also used to prevent water seepage in the areas around sinks, where floor tile meets baseboard tile, and around tile soap holders.

Helpful Tiling Tools

Most of the tools required for installing tile, whether ceramic, resilient, or wood, are general purpose tools you may already have. You'll recognize most of those illustrated on the opposite page. A few are tools used specifically for ceramic tile work.

A notched trowel for spreading adhesive is essential for any tiling project. Be sure to buy one with properly sized notches for your project.

For ceramic tile installation, you'll need a snap cutter to cut tile quickly and accurately. This can be rented, but some dealers lend them out. You'll need tile nippers to cut and shape curved lines on tile. These are inexpensive and available at hardware stores.

For applying grout between ceramic tiles, purchase a rubber-backed trowel.

Use a caulking gun to apply silicone caulk, and a cold chisel if necessary to break out old tile. If you need to scrape a floor clean of old tile and mastic, you can rent a floor scraper.

To cut holes in tile, use a concrete drill bit to make the hole, and then do the cutting with a rod saw that fits in a hacksaw. Special tile-cutting saw blades that fit saber saws are also usually available at the tile dealer.

A sliding bevel square is useful if you have to transfer corners to tile. For matching irregular shapes, use a contour gauge. An abrasive stone is used to buff tile edges smooth after they have been cut.

A hammer, tape measure, square, and crosscut saw are needed to install new backing.

A rubber mallet is handy to bed tiles into the adhesive, but you can also use a padded wood block with a hammer.

When laying resilient tiles, cut the tile with a utility knife guided by a square. Use a nail punch to set nails flush with the subfloor.

Helpful Tiling Tools

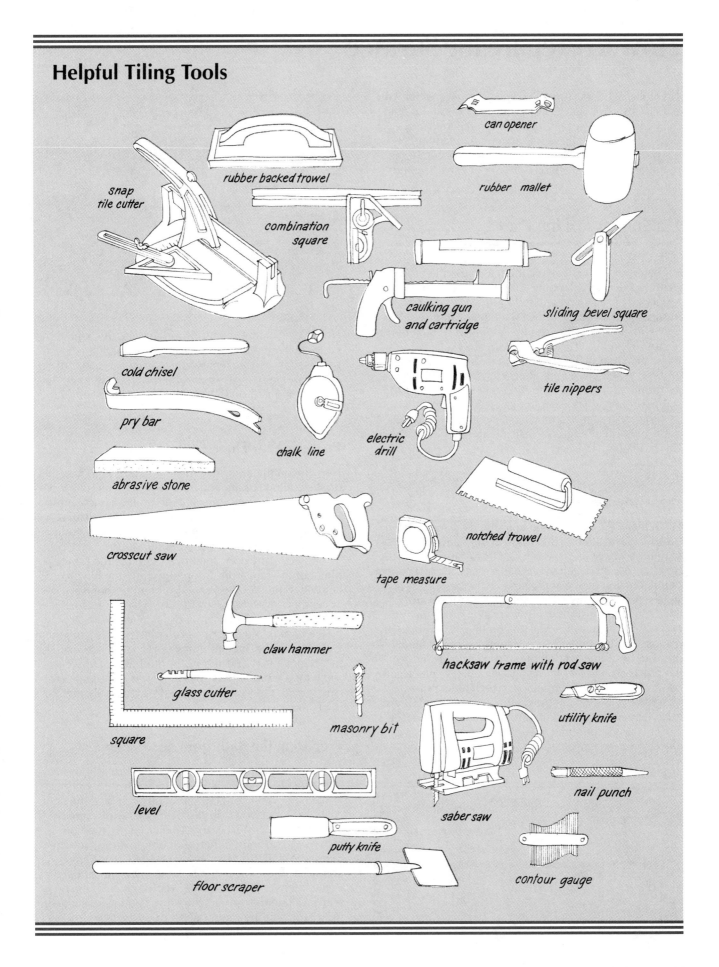

can opener

rubber backed trowel

rubber mallet

snap tile cutter

combination square

caulking gun and cartridge

sliding bevel square

cold chisel

chalk line

electric drill

tile nippers

pry bar

abrasive stone

notched trowel

crosscut saw

tape measure

claw hammer

hacksaw frame with rod saw

glass cutter

utility knife

square

masonry bit

level

saber saw

nail punch

putty knife

floor scraper

contour gauge

How to Prepare the Surface

No matter which ceramic tile you choose or where you plan to install it, successful results require careful planning and meticulous preparation. On the following pages you'll find helpful information on planning your tile project as well as a guide to the selection, use, and preparation of the backing—the surface that supports the tile.

Making a Working Plan

Whether or not you hire a contractor, your tile project requires thorough planning. Start by outlining the sequence of steps you will follow. Involve your family in this; they will have to live with the disruptions, but they will also enjoy the results. An understanding family is most important if your project involves a large high-traffic area that will be worked on in stages over a period of days. Whether you are tiling a kitchen, bath, or family room, your family's life style will be disrupted to some extent and you should plan accordingly.

To prepare the working area, clear away rugs, furniture, and anything else that might get in the way. Cover adjacent finished areas with paper or plastic sheeting.

Preparing for Wall Tiles

Wash the walls with a good household cleaner, such as trisodium phosphate (TSP, available in hardware stores) to remove grease film, which can impair the adhesive. Baseboards can be left in place to support the first course of tile, but you may want to remove the baseboard and shoe molding, if any. Most moldings and trims are attached with finishing nails; you can remove them in two ways. One way is to hammer a thin, broad-bladed pry bar gently behind the molding and pry carefully outward until that section of molding is loose. Repeat the process a few feet farther along until that piece can be removed. The other method, which reduces the chances of splitting the molding, is to find the nails and drive them through the molding with a narrow nailset.

You need not remove window or door casing; just tile up to it, leaving enough space for a grout joint.

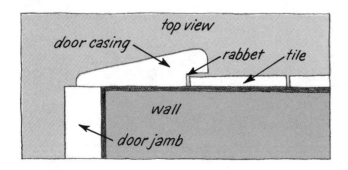

However, in some situations running the tile behind the casing will eliminate an awkward tile cut. If this is necessary, carefully remove the casing and then cut a rabbet in the back as shown below to allow room for the tile. You can do this neatly with a router or table saw.

Preparing for Floor Tiles

New tile on the floor may mean you'll have to trim the doors to allow for the added height. To determine where the door must be cut, place a tile on the floor against the door and mark. Allow an additional ⅛" clearance for inside doors. On exterior doors allow for weather-stripping on the bottom edge of the door.

Remove any doors that open into the room by tapping out the hinge pins (don't unscrew the hinges) and cut with a fine-toothed saw. To minimize splintering, cover the cutline on both sides with masking tape.

If removing the baseboards is difficult (which may be the case in older homes with plaster walls) and there is quarter-round shoe molding next to the baseboard, just remove that and tile up to the baseboard. Leave room for a grout joint between the tile and baseboard. Any irregularities can be covered when the shoe molding is replaced.

Preparing the Bathroom or Kitchen

You may need to remove accessories such as towel bars and paper holders from the walls. For bathroom floors, remove the vanity or pedestal wash basin and the floor-mounted toilet bowl. To tile bathroom walls, remove wall-mounted basins or toilets. (For information on removing and reinstalling plumbing fixtures, see the *Sunset* book *Basic Plumbing Illustrated*.) For tiling around a shower or bathtub, remove the faucet handles, escutcheons, spigots, and shower heads. Line the tub with cardboard to protect the finish and to prevent debris from clogging the drain. Wrap masking tape around any exposed pipe threads.

Backings:
The Foundation for Ceramic Tile

Of all the steps in successful tile installation, probably the most important is preparing the backing, the material over which the tile will be placed. A thorough job of installing or preparing the backing will save you time and money later. Backings must be solid, flat, clean, and dry. Don't try to install tile over a springy surface. If the surface gives under pressure, replace it or cover it with a smooth, rigid surface. Any movement will cause the grout and tile to crack. The chart below shows the limits of an irregular surface, as recommended by the Tile Council of America. If your backing doesn't come within these limits, you may be able either to sand out the bumps or to fill the dips with epoxy adhesive, which dries hard and smooth.

To check a floor for dips, run a long straightedge over the floor and look at it against the light for gaps under the board. Mark the outer edges of the dip with pencil and then fill by troweling in an epoxy. After the epoxy has dried, use an abrasive stone to smooth out the filler along the edges. If the surface is very irregular, cover or replace it.

Surface	Adhesive	Must be flat within
All walls	All thin-sets	$\frac{1}{8}$" in 8'
Concrete floor	Thin-set and epoxy	$\frac{1}{8}$" in 10'
	Mastic	$\frac{1}{8}$" in 3'
Wood floor*	Epoxy	$\frac{1}{8}$" in 10'
	Mastic	$\frac{1}{16}$" in 3'

*Adjacent edges of plywood subfloors must not be above or below each other by more than $\frac{1}{32}$".

Ceramic tiles can be laid on a variety of existing backings. If the old backing is unsatisfactory, one of several new backings may be used. These materials and their installation or preparation are described below.

New Backings

If you're going to install a new backing for your tile work, you have several materials to choose from. Your choice will depend on where and how the tile will be used. Possible new backings include plywood, gypsum wallboard, backer board, concrete slab, waterproof membrane, and mortar bed.

Plywood. Plywood is the most commonly used backing for floors and countertops. It can be used to cover old, uneven floors or kitchen floors that have either old vinyl asbestos tiles (which should not be torn up because of the asbestos fibers) or cushioned vinyl tiles (which are too springy for ceramic tile backing). Exterior grade plywood, which has water-resistant glues, should always be used. (Plywood with "X" in its grade marking,

as in ACX, means "exterior.") Most other wood backing, such as planks or tongue-and-groove boards, may not be smooth or strong enough. Floors and countertops should not flex once the tile is down or grout and tile may crack.

For tile floors, most professionals insist that the thickness of the subfloor and finished floor combined be 1¼". This is the thickness of the tongue-and-groove plywood commonly used for subfloors in recent construction. If your floor backing is not this thick, then add sufficient exterior grade plywood. If you're not sure how thick your subfloor is (older houses often have ¾" boards), drill a hole in the floor and measure. A floor any less thick is too subject to flexing.

When putting down plywood over existing plywood subfloors, place the new wood so that the middle of the panel falls over and covers the butted ends of the existing plywood. Stagger the new panels so that the four corners do not line up (see page 69). Leave a slight gap, about ⅟₃₂", between adjacent panels to permit expansion. Nail panels to the subfloor with ring-shank nails twice as long as the new plywood is thick. Space the nails 6" apart along the edges and 12" apart in the field, where you should follow the floor joists if possible.

For countertops, use ¼" exterior plywood. Make sure it is firmly supported by the cabinets and is screwed into the top edges of the cabinet every 12". On counters or floors that may get wet, the preferred adhesive for plywood is epoxy; on normal floors use mastic.

Gypsum wallboard. Also called drywall, gypsum wallboard is a common backing for ceramic tiles on walls. But because the gypsum core disintegrates if it becomes damp, standard gypsum wallboard (which has a gray

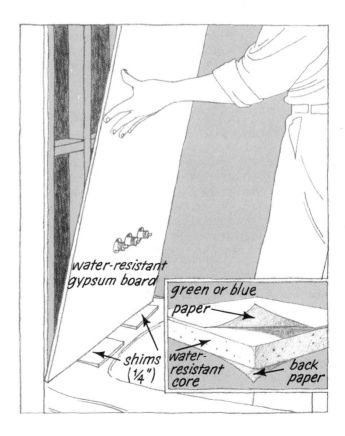

water-resistant gypsum board

green or blue paper

shims (¼")

water-resistant core

back paper

paper covering) should never be used in wet areas. Most new bathrooms are covered with a water-resistant gypsum wallboard, which has a green or blue paper covering. Use an epoxy adhesive and seal the grout, and you should have no water penetration.

To install, use nails or adhesive to fasten gypsum wallboard to existing walls or studs. Tape corners and joints and cover the nail heads. Use cement-base or mastic adhesives for ceramic tile on gypsum wallboard.

Water-resistant gypsum board should be applied directly to the studs with nails or adhesive. Using special joint compound according to the instructions of the gypsum board manufacturer, tape all joints between panels, cover all nail heads, and seal all cut edges. With this type of gypsum wallboard, use mastic, which is water-resistant, for setting the tile.

Backer board. Backer board is technically called concrete glassfiber-reinforced backer board. Essentially a thin piece of concrete sandwiched between pieces of fiberglass mesh, this relatively new material combines the waterproof qualities of mortar and the easy installation of drywall. It can be used to cover existing gypsum wallboard to prevent water penetration; it won't disintegrate or swell if it gets wet.

Backer board, usually in panels 7/16" thick and ranging in size from 3' by 4' to 3' by 6', is fastened with 1½" galvanized roofing nails or screws directly to the wall studs or over existing drywall. Seal joints between panels and between panel and tub or shower receptor, as well as any other openings, with a cement-base adhesive. Tape corners with 2"-wide coated fiberglass tape embedded in a thin coat of mortar. Use either thin-set or epoxy as the tile adhesive.

Cement backer boards can also be installed over plywood subfloors if additional waterproofing is needed. They will not support any load by themselves on a horizontal surface. For maximum resistance to flexing, glue the backer boards to the subfloor with a cement-base adhesive and then nail every 6" with 1½" galvanized roofing nails. Fill gaps between the panels with the same adhesive used to set the tiles.

Concrete slab. A concrete slab is an excellent base for ceramic tiles, both indoors and out. The concrete must be completely cured, free from waxy or oily films, and free of any concrete dust. Any cracks or holes must be filled with concrete patching material, available at most hardware stores. The concrete floor must stay dry year-round. To check it, conduct the simple test on page 45.

In pouring a new slab for a tile base, be sure to place a plastic vapor barrier between the slab and the ground, and reinforce the slab thoroughly to prevent any cracking. Finish the slab with a light brooming to give it a slightly rough texture, which will make the adhesive bond very well to the slab. The preferred adhesive is thin-set, the cement-base adhesive.

Waterproof membrane. This is a means of waterproofing a wall instead of covering it with backer board or replacing it. Waterproof membrane, which comes in a kit, consists of fiberglass mesh and light tar. To apply, first cut the fabric to fit the wall in a vertical section.

Roll on a thin layer of tar and then roll the piece of mesh into the tar. Cut a second piece of mesh to fit at a right angle over the first piece and roll it into the tar. Apply a second layer of tar and let dry.

Mortar bed. Mortar bed is the traditional backing for tile. Its value is that curves, and therefore coves, can be built into counters or around sinks to give the tile a unique look. If you want this, consider having an experienced professional lay the mortar bed to your specifications and then tile it yourself.

Existing Backings

You can install ceramic tile directly over many existing backings, such as old tile, linoleum, sheet vinyl floors, smooth plaster, brick, plywood, and concrete.

Be sure that the surfaces are sound, clean, flat, (see chart on page 43), and properly prepared. Make certain that you use the correct adhesive. If the existing surface is badly cracked or broken, loose, irregular, or otherwise in poor condition, replace it or cover with a new backing.

Gypsum wallboard. This is the most common existing wall surface. Generally, it need only be clean and free of wallpaper, which heavy tile will pull loose. In bathrooms, use the water-resistant wallboard—not standard wallboard. If the wallboard is damaged, mildewed, or crumbly, it absolutely must be torn out and replaced with a new backing.

Clean dirt and grease from gypsum board walls with a cleaner such as TSP. Remove any loose or flaking paint with a wire brush; roughen the finish if it is glossy. Sanding will do both jobs. Fill any cracks, gouges, or holes with a drywall patching compound. Remove any wallpaper from the wallboard. Use mastic or epoxy to bond ceramic tiles to existing gypsum wallboard.

Wood surfaces. Whether floor or wall, the surface must be very smooth, and this generally means using plywood. On floors the subfloor must be 1¼" thick to prevent flexing, which can crack tile and grout. Add additional plywood if necessary. Plank surfaces in most cases are not smooth enough and should be covered with plywood. However, if the planks are smooth enough to tile over, clean the surface. If there is a polyurethane or shellac coating, roughen it with a wire brush to make the adhesive stick better.

Resilient floors. This includes a variety of materials, as you will see in the chapter "Resilient Tile." These floors make good backings if smooth, clean, and tightly in place. But cushioned vinyl, a common sheet vinyl covering, is not a good backing because it allows some flexing, which cracks grout and tile. Cushioned vinyl floors can be covered with 3/8" exterior plywood, using the guidelines on page 69.

To lay ceramic tile over a vinyl or linoleum floor, use epoxy adhesive or a good mastic. Be sure that the floor is 1¼" thick, drilling a small hole to check if necessary.

Another reminder: Your sheet vinyl floor may be

vinyl asbestos, which is no longer on the market. Don't sand it or tear it up because this will put dangerous asbestos fibers into the air. It must be covered over.

Concrete subfloor. An existing concrete subfloor must be flat, smooth, dry, clean, and free of cracks. Remove grease and oil stains with a chemical garage floor cleaner, available at most auto supply stores. Chip or scrape off any excess concrete, paint, or other foreign material. If the concrete surface is glossy, effloresced, sealed, or painted, roughen it by sanding with a rented floor sander fitted with #4 or #5 open-cut sandpaper. Finish by vacuuming up all loose material and then damp-mopping up the dust.

Fill all the holes, low areas, cracks, and expansion joints with a good concrete patching material or with the thin-set adhesive you'll use for the tile. The floor must be flat (see chart on page 43).

If your concrete floor is rough, uneven, or otherwise in poor condition, consider having a new concrete surface poured over it.

Ceramic tile. Existing ceramic tile may be used as backing for new ceramic tiles. But make sure the old tile is in good condition, well bonded, and clean.

Loose tiles are signs of trouble. They often mean water has penetrated the grout or has leaked in from behind and weakened the backing. Remove any loose tiles and examine the backing; be aggressive and pull off any tile that is suspect. It is easier to replace a questionable tile at this point than to do the job over later. If there's no problem, clean the old adhesive from the tile and backing, and replace with new adhesive. If you find damp gypsum board behind wall tiles, remove all the tile and replace the old backing.

Where there are many loose or broken tiles, it is best to remove all of them. If the old tile is on a plywood-backed countertop, use a cold chisel and hammer—and safety goggles—to break it out; then scrape and sand the surface until smooth. It may be easier to apply a new top. For walls, pull out the drywall and tile together, and install either waterproof drywall or cement backer board for the new backing. Be sure to protect the shower or tub area against scratches or chips.

If you must place new tile over old, clean it thoroughly to remove scum, mineral buildup, coatings, wax, and dirt. Use a belt sander or an abrasive disk mounted on an electric drill. Both will also roughen the old tile and make the adhesive bond better. Wear a good dust mask as you work and remove all dust after you finish.

One more factor to consider in planning the new tile is whether to stop at the height of the existing tile or to continue up to the ceiling. If stopping with the old tile, cover the edge with a cove and bullnose cap. To tile to the ceiling, install new backing above the old. Shim the backing if necessary to make it flush with the old tile. In damp areas, use water-resistant gypsum board or cement backer board.

You may use any of the thin-set adhesives or epoxy described on page 39 over existing tile.

Priming or Sealing Your Backing

Good insurance for your tile work means first applying a sealer to the backing, even with exterior grade plywood. This inexpensive step minimizes the chance of water penetration. Sealer (sometimes known as bonderizer) accomplishes two things on backings: it increases water resistance and strengthens the bond between backing and tile.

The sealer may be a thin coat of the adhesive or a special material prepared by the adhesive manufacturer. Read the label on your adhesive container for information on sealers.

Is Your Concrete Floor Dry?

A flat, interior concrete slab makes an excellent backing for all types of tile— as long as it remains dry. A damp slab causes most tile adhesives to deteriorate and makes resilient and wood tiles swell, buckle, or rot. Although the builder may have waterproofed the slab by placing a polyethylene barrier on the ground before pouring the concrete, you generally can't be sure of this. Unless such a vapor barrier is present, moisture can be drawn up through the concrete to the surface.

The best time to check a slab for dampness is just after a rainstorm, when the ground is saturated with water. To make the test, place several 1' squares of plastic (bread wrappers will do) on the slab. Tape all edges down to trap any moisture.

After 24 hours, check the squares. If the undersides are fogged with moisture, the slab is too wet to lay tile on.

If persistent moisture is evident, call in professional help. The Yellow Pages are a good source. For resilient or wood tile work, look under "Floor Laying, Refinishing, & Resurfacing." For ceramic tile work, look under "Tile—Ceramic, Contractors." If the bases of the walls and the slab are wet, your problem may be serious enough to require a waterproofing specialist. See the listings under "Waterproofing Contractors" or "Concrete Contractors."

Here are four solutions for keeping your slab's surface dry:

1) Lay a drain tile in a ditch around your house.

2) Lay a sheet of polyethylene on top of your slab and cover it with another concrete slab at least 1" thick.

3) If you're installing parquet, spread "cold applied cutback asphalt" across the slab, and then press overlapping polyethylene strips into the asphalt.

4) Trowel a commercially prepared latex-base waterproofing compound onto the slab. However, these compounds are generally unavailable to homeowners for do-it-yourself application.

How to Install Ceramic Tile

On the preceding pages you have learned what kinds of tile are available; where tile is appropriate; how to plan for, select, and buy tile; how to prepare various backings; which kinds of adhesives to use; and which kinds of grout to apply. This section will take you through some basic tiling projects and finishing touches.

A Few Pointers

Here are some tips that apply to any of the ceramic tiling projects discussed.

Testing Your Layout

You'll have to adapt each project to your own unique situation. For this reason, always make a dry run by laying out tiles on the surface you are covering. If that surface is vertical, mark out a similar area on the floor. This will help you anticipate any problems, decide where to cut tiles, and locate the trim pieces. Always arrange the tile layout so the cut tiles are in the least noticeable corners.

When using a mixture of decorative and plain tiles, be sure the decorative tiles are high enough to be visible and aren't hidden behind furniture.

Planning the Sequence

If you intend to install tile both on walls and on floors, as in a bathroom, tile all the walls before the floor. This is necessary if you are using cove tile at the bottom of the wall. Even if you are not using coves, this sequence is still more convenient. For walls, start with the tub enclosure (the wall area around the tub).

Applying the Adhesive

The directions supplied by the manufacturer of your adhesive will tell you how the material should be mixed and what size notches the trowel should have to produce the correct thickness of the adhesive layer. They'll also give you the open time (the length of time you have to work with the adhesive after spreading it). You commonly have 30 minutes to an hour. However, be aware that epoxy must be applied when the temperature is between 60° and 90°. In hot weather epoxy goes on more easily but sets up more quickly; the opposite is true in cold weather.

All the adhesives—thin-set, mastic, or epoxy—are applied in basically the same way. Start by pouring a small amount of adhesive (two or three cups) on the floor backing. For a wall, dip the adhesive from the container with your trowel. As you become more familiar with the process, you can cover larger areas. Using the notched edge of the trowel to form a thin layer,

spread the adhesive over the backing. Keep the trowel at about a 30° angle to the surface, and press it firmly against the backing to form ridges in the adhesive. Work back and forth in a cross-hatch pattern.

A few more tips: Spread only the amount of adhesive you can comfortably reach over. With button back tiles, use a deep enough layer of adhesive to ensure they're properly bedded. And if you're using a mastic with a solvent base, remember to ventilate the working area well.

Spacing the Tiles

Some tiles have small protrusions which serve as built-in spacers (lugs), but floor tiles and many wall tiles must be individually spaced apart and aligned. By far the simplest method for spacing is to use the molded plastic spacers available from your dealer. They come in a wide variety of sizes to fit many needs. These spacers should be used as shown in the illustration on page 32. They must be removed before the grout is applied. You can also use scraps of plywood (see page 49), which work well with ¼" or wider joints. For the narrower joints sometimes associated with wall tiles, use finishing nails if spacers are not available (see page 53). Tiles can also be spaced and aligned by using cord or rope pulled tight between two nails at the ends of each course. Use nylon to avoid fibers sticking in the adhesive. Still another method, usable for joints of any size, is to use a tile stick, as shown on page 48.

Mosaics come already spaced and mounted on a mesh backing. Lay down 1 or 2 square feet of these tiles at a time, adding spacing only between each new section put down.

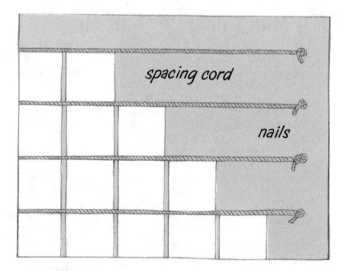

Spacing tiles *in traditional way uses cord or rope. As you set each course, lay damp cord of desired size on top of tiles. Secure cord by wrapping end around nail. Remove cord and nails after adhesive sets.*

Marking & Cutting Ceramic Tiles

Whatever your tile project, you will undoubtedly have to cut tile, and to cut it in various ways: straight, curved, at angles, or with holes.

Though tile dealers will cut tile for you with a diamond saw, repeated trips to the dealer are impractical, especially if your tiling job is complicated. Even though tiles are thick and hard, you can cut them without too much difficulty. You just need the right tools, as shown on page 41. Your dealer may lend you the tools, or you can rent them.

Marking the cut. If your tiles have ridged backs, make cuts parallel to the ridges. To mark for straight cuts, place the tile, finished surface up, exactly

on top of the last full tile you set (see page 78). Then place another tile on top of this one, with one edge butted against the wall. Using the edge of the top tile as a guide, mark the cut-off line with a fine felt-tip pen.

To mark a tile for a corner, use this process twice—once on each wall.

To fit a tile to an irregular contour, match it with a contour gauge and transfer the outline to the tile with a felt-tip pen. You can also cut a pattern from cardboard and then transfer the shape to the tile.

Where a pipe comes through the wall, as in tubs and showers, place all the other field tiles first. Then either

measure the location of the required hole or hold the tile against the pipe and mark the hole (see drawing on page 57). The escutcheons will hide any minor inaccuracies. To cut the hole, see the drawings below.

Cutting tile. Shown below are the common methods of cutting tile. When using tile nippers, don't try to cut the first time on the line; cut short of it and then carefully nibble up. Too big a bite the first time usually results in chipping beyond the line.

Smoothing edges. After a tile is snapped or nipped, remove any rough edges with an abrasive stone or piece of concrete.

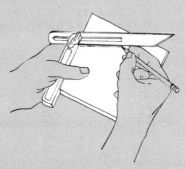

A sliding bevel square *can duplicate any angle. Adjust the blade to the area to be filled and transfer the angle to the tile.*

To fit tile *against an irregular outline, use a contour gauge to find the outline, trace it on the tile, and then cut with nippers.*

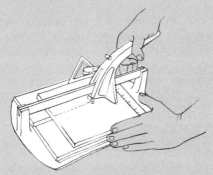

On the cutter, *position the tile and then score the surface by pulling the handle toward you while pressing down firmly.*

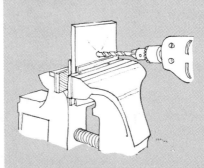

To cut a hole *in tile, first drill through it with a masonry bit. If the tile is held in a vise, protect it with a piece of scrap wood on each side.*

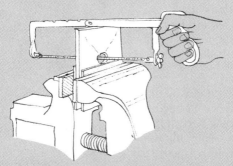

After the hole is drilled, *pass the rod saw (a cutting cable available at your dealer) through the hole and hook it to your hacksaw. If you don't have a vise, clamp the tile to the edge of a table, protecting the tile with pieces of wood.*

Use tile nippers *to cut both irregular shapes and narrow straight lines. If a narrow edge of tile must be cut in a straight line, first score the tile with the snap cutter; for irregular or curved lines, score the line with a glass cutter. Then nibble your way up to the line.*

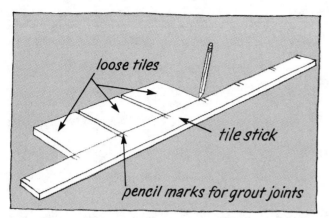

Tile stick *with a straightedge can be used to lay and space tiles. Use 1" by 3" or 1" by 4" lumber marked with proper spacing for grout joints.*

Installing Tiles on the Floor

Floors are among the easier tiling projects for the do-it-yourselfer. Because the tiles are set on a horizontal surface, gravity is on your side—their weight holds the tiles in place. This section gives you some preparation reminders and discusses laying out the job, setting the tiles, and adding the finishing touches.

Preparation

Before you begin, be sure to read the section on preparing the surface (see page 42). The backing for a ceramic tile floor must be rigid, flat, smooth, clean, and dry.

Materials. Check the tiles, adhesives, and grout you purchased. Do the tile colors match from box to box? Slight variations are one of the charms of tile, but you may prefer uniformity. Is the adhesive compatible with your backing? Will the grout work with the adhesive and tiles you have? Answer these questions now.

Many tiles, particularly those with reddish bodies, tend to be dusty. This dust can prevent adhesives from bonding to the tiles. If necessary, brush them clean with a wire brush before use.

Plan for doorways. Where tile ends in a doorway or similar opening, there is often a difference in height between the tile surface and the adjoining floor. If the tile is higher, you can finish off the edge with bullnose tiles. These have a curved edge that creates a smooth transition between the two levels. When a tile floor meets a carpeted area, the levels may be roughly the same, so regular square-edge tiles may do the job. With mosaic tile, a marble threshold (available from your dealer) is often used to make a transition between two levels.

Marking the Working Lines

Working lines are laid out on the subfloor to keep your first tile courses straight and to adjust for any crooked-

ness in the room walls. Laying out accurate working lines for the first courses of tile seems tedious, but doing this job right will make the rest go faster and smoother. Also, this is the time to decide on the tile bond, or pattern; the joints can all be lined up (known as jack-on-jack) or the rows can be staggered, as in the running bond pattern of the quarry tile floor shown on page 8. Both are illustrated on page 53. Take the time to plan carefully.

Two basic methods are used to establish working lines. In one, a chalk line (available at hardware stores) is snapped down the center of the room; in the other, lines are snapped near a wall. If you have picked tiles that are not square or rectangular, such as ogee or Moorish, you may have to make some adjustments in the working lines. Make a dry run before you open the adhesive.

Working from the center. If your room is out of square or if your decorative design or pattern should be symmetrically located in the room, you'll probably want to start in the center. The layout of working lines and the tiling sequence for this method are described on pages 69–70. Nail wood battens along the working lines to help keep the tiles straight. This method usually means having cut tiles along all four walls.

Starting at the wall. Many professional tile setters use this method. Its roots are in the traditional way of setting tiles, in which tile setters worked from one end to avoid disturbing the carefully leveled mortar bed. This method usually means that tiles will have to be cut along two walls. Plan to put the rows of cut tiles where they'll be least noticeable.

If you start tiling against a wall that's out of square, the last course of tile along the opposite wall may have to be cut progressively wider or narrower. To avoid this, correct the room's layout and squareness using the following method.

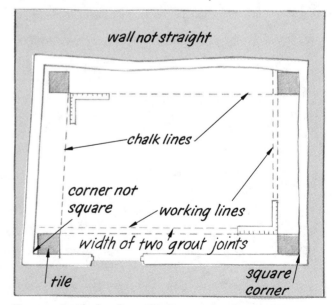

You can start laying floor tiles *from one wall even if corners are not square or wall not straight. When two adjacent walls are straight and form a square corner, you'll find job easier.*

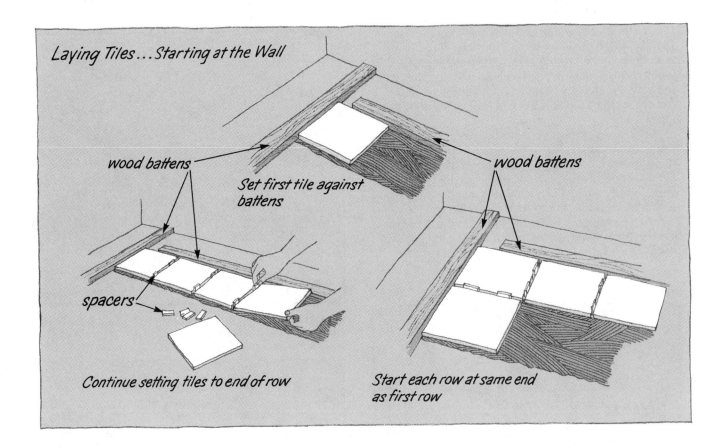

Laying Tiles...Starting at the Wall

wood battens

Set first tile against battens

wood battens

spacers

Continue setting tiles to end of row

Start each row at same end as first row

Check the room for square corners and straight walls by placing a tile firmly against the wall in each corner of the room. Snap a chalk line along the outside edges of the tiles from one corner to the next. Variations in the distance between chalk line and wall will show any crookedness in the wall. Variations about the width of a grout joint can be tolerated. Baseboards and shoe molding can also cover some irregularities. Using a framing square, see if the lines at any corner intersect at right angles. The easiest place to start is from a straight wall that adjoins a square corner.

Before you start to mark your working lines, make a dry run—laying the tile out on the floor—to help determine the best layout and minimize the number of cut tiles. Use spacers for the grout lines. A tile stick (see page 48) can also help you achieve uniform spacing. Sometimes a slight alteration of grout joint widths can eliminate a row of cut tiles. Try to place cut tiles so furniture can help hide them.

Whether you've started from the center or at one wall, after you've snapped lines to determine the straightness of the walls, you next lay out the working lines. Start by using the chalked lines on the floor as a guide. Your working lines should allow for slight variations in the straightness of the walls (about the width of a grout joint) and for the grout joint between the first and second rows of tiles. Select the walls you wish to use as guides and pick one of them to begin on. Then, on the side of the line away from the wall, mark another line parallel to the first and spaced a distance equal to the width of two grout joints Repeat this with the chalk line along the other wall. These are your working lines.

Nail a wood batten (1" by 2" or 1" by 3") along each of the working lines. These will give you ridged guides to butt the tiles against. Make sure the battens in a corner form a right angle. If they don't, check your measurements and adjust as needed.

Laying the Tiles

Now you're ready to start putting ceramic tiles on the floor. Spread a strip of adhesive on the floor along one of the battens with the notched trowel recommended by your adhesive manufacturer. Spread only a few square feet at a time, usually an area 2' by 4', until you become familiar with the process. In a larger area, some adhesive may dry before you can place the tile.

Place the first tile with a gentle rocking motion into the corner formed by the two battens. Never slide tile on the adhesive; it pushes the adhesive up between the joints. Make sure the tile is butted tightly against the wood guides. With the same motion, place the second tile alongside the first, against the spacers. Floor tiles seldom have molded-in spacers, so use a few molded spacers or pieces of properly sized wood to establish the width of the grout joint. The molded spacers are best used by pushing one end into the joint and leaving the rest sticking up for easy removal. It's not necessary to fit them into the corners between each tile. Remove any spacers after the adhesive begins to set. As you go along, clean off any adhesive that gets on the surface of the tiles. This is especially important with epoxy, which is hard to remove after it dries.

(Continued on next page)

. . . Continued from page 49

Continue setting tiles and spacers along the batten until you reach the other end of the room. If necessary, mark and cut the last tile as described on page 47. If you're using a running bond pattern, just start the second row—and every other row thereafter—with the first tile spaced one-half the width of a tile from the batten guide.

Whichever pattern you choose, begin each new row from the same side of the room as the first one. Measure and cut the last tile as required. After you have laid a section, the tiles should be bedded in. Do this with a rubber mallet or by hammering lightly on a block of padded wood large enough to cover several tiles at once. This process sets the tile firmly in the adhesive and levels each with the others. In moving the padded block about, be careful not to push a tile out of line.

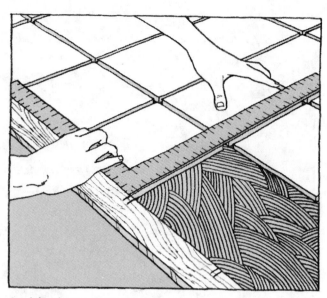

Straightedge *marked with tile spacing will help you maintain straight courses and even spacings. Check with square often to assure professional look.*

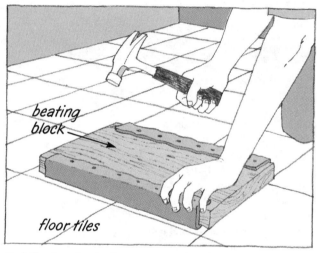

Bed tiles *in adhesive by tapping on length of padded lumber or plywood while sliding it over tiles. Smooth, even surface results.*

Try to stay off the surface of the tiles as you work. When you get to the last few rows, you'll have to reposition yourself onto the tiles. Lay down pieces of plywood over the tiles to distribute your weight.

From time to time, check with a square and straightedge to make sure the courses are straight. If some of the tiles are out of line, don't panic. Just wiggle them back into position.

After you set the last row, begin laying the border tiles in the same corner you started in. Carefully remove the battens and spread adhesive in the areas not yet tiled. Work toward the ends, using spacers and bedding the tiles as you move along. If you laid out your working lines properly, you won't have to cut these tiles. You will have grout line spaces on both sides. When you've finished, clean off the surface of the tiles.

Stay off the tiles at least overnight—longer if recommended by the adhesive manufacturer. To keep tiles from breaking, keep all but essential traffic off the floor until you grout the joints. After the adhesive has fully set (see page 62), you can begin grouting.

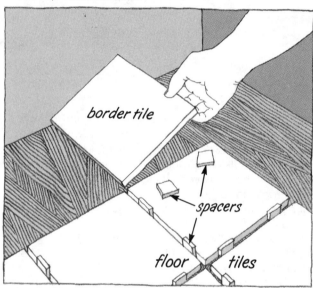

After main part *of floor is tiled, carefully remove battens. Spread adhesive on remaining floor and set border tiles.*

Finishing Up

Wait until the adhesive dries before applying grout (see page 62). Remove any remaining spacers, clean adhesive from the tile surface, and reread the information about grouts beginning on page 40. Also remove any excess adhesive or debris from the joints; otherwise, the grout may crack or fail to bond in those areas. After the adhesive has dried, apply the grout as described on page 62.

When the grout is fully cured, wash the surface with detergent or household cleaner and a small amount of water. When your new tile floor is completely dry, seal the grout as described on page 63.

If necessary, cut door bottoms and reinstall the doors. After the grout has dried, replace the baseboards and any molding.

Installing Tile on Walls

Decorating a straight wall with ceramic tile is relatively easy. If your wall has breaks or openings, the job will require cutting some tile. But proceed carefully and methodically and you'll create a tiled wall that will give you pleasure for many years.

Preparation

Remove faceplates for electrical switches and outlets, bathroom accessories, and anything else attached to the wall.

If the area you're tiling contains any electrical outlets or switches, you must move the outlets forward until they are flush with the new wall. There are two ways to do this. The simplest, which works in most cases, is to use some small washers. Turn power off to the switch or receptacle, unscrew the faceplate, and check that power is off with a circuit tester (available for a few dollars at hardware stores). If it is a receptacle, test with a lamp. Note that the switch or receptacle is held in the box by two screws, top and bottom. Unscrew these, pull the device forward, and slip small washers over the screw between the box and device. Use enough washers to bring the device out flush with the new wall. The other way, if you need to bring the box forward an inch or more, is to use box extenders (available at your hardware store). These extenders screw on to the existing switch box; the switch or receptacle is then screwed back onto the extender.

If your project includes adding electrical outlets or installing a recessed cabinet, now is the time to do the work inside the wall. The *Sunset* books *Basic Carpentry Illustrated* and *Basic Home Wiring Illustrated* provide valuable information for these projects.

The wall surface must be firm, dry, clean, and flat. It can be of any of the materials described under "Existing Backings" on page 44. Remove any wallpaper; it may loosen and peel off, taking your new tiles with it. Be sure to clean off dirt and grease and roughen shiny areas. Painted surfaces are acceptable as long as the paint is not flaking. If the surface seems porous, follow the recommendations of the adhesive manufacturer regarding priming or sealing.

Marking the Working Lines

Accurate working lines help keep the tiles properly aligned, giving your completed tile work an elegant and professional look. Two working lines, horizontal and vertical, must be established to ensure that your first rows, or courses, are straight.

The horizontal line. This line makes the first, or bottom, course of tile level, even if the floor isn't. The line is usually established near the floor. However, if you are tiling around a tub enclosure, see the section on this procedure on page 54.

Find the floor's lowest point by setting the level on the floor at various locations against the walls to be tiled. At the lowest point, place a tile against the wall (see drawing below); mark its top edge on the wall. If the installation will have a cove base, set a cove tile on the floor and a wall tile above it. Use spacers to include the grout joint. Mark the top of the wall tile and the second grout joint. Using the level and a long straightedge, draw a horizontal line from this point across the wall. Continue it along all walls to be tiled, but double-check your work; it is easy to get a little off level.

After marking your horizontal working lines, nail batten (1" by 3" lengths will do) to the walls. Their top edges should be on the lines.

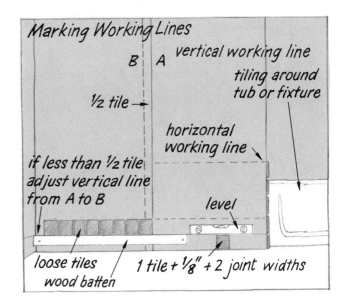

The vertical lines. Measure to find the midpoint of a wall and mark it on the horizontal line (see drawing above). Starting at this midpoint, measure with the tile stick or set a row of loose tiles on the batten to determine the size of the tiles at each end of the wall. Don't forget the spacers. If the end tiles will be less than half a tile, move your midpoint mark one-half tile to avoid narrow pieces at each end. Then use the level and straightedge to mark a vertical line on the wall through the mark. Repeat the process with the other walls.

Some final hints. If you don't plan to tile all the way to the ceiling, mark where you want to stop. Usually a tile wainscot extends to a height between 4' and 5'. With your tile stick, mark the top of the uppermost tile on your vertical line, including the bullnose or cap tile (a half bullnose). With your level, mark a horizontal line through this point across the wall. Repeat the process for the other walls.

For bathroom walls, lay out the locations of ceramic towel bars, paper holders, and soap and toothbrush holders. Mark them on the backing and cut tile to fit around the marks, allowing for grout lines. These accessories must be installed later because they are heavy and must be taped in place until the adhesive dries. To install a grab bar in a tub or shower enclosure, locate and mark the center of the appropriate wall studs with pencil marks on the ceiling before you tile. After

(Continued on page 53)

Replacing Damaged Tiles

If one of your tiles is damaged, you can replace it by following steps 1 through 9. Often, however, you may find several loose tiles. This may indicate more serious problems with the backing. Check carefully. Don't be afraid to pull off a tile that is only a little loose now; it will get worse. If the backing looks all right, the problem may be with the adhesive. Clean as shown below and replace. Wear safety goggles for this work.

Resetting loose tiles. Start by scraping all traces of adhesive and grout from the tile and the backing surface. Then follow steps 5 through 9.

Matching replacement tiles. If you don't have a spare tile from the original set, you may have trouble finding an exact match. Check dealers' bone piles of odds and ends or put in a decorative tile. When looking for replacements, carry along a sample of the original tile, if possible.

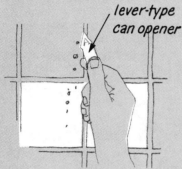

Step 1. Remove grout from joints around damaged tile with a lever-type can opener.

Step 2. Punch hole through center of damaged tile with hammer and nail set or large nail. Be careful not to damage the surface behind.

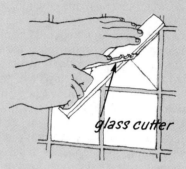

Step 3. With a glass cutter, score a deep X across the face of the tile, through the center hole.

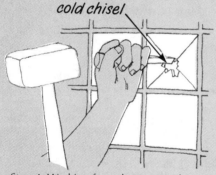

Step 4. Working from the center, chip out the old tile and remaining grout with hammer and cold chisel, using light, rapid blows.

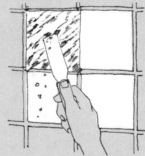

Step 5. Clean area behind tile with chisel, removing old adhesive and grout. Smooth rough edges with sandpaper.

Step 6. If backing is damaged, fill and smooth with patching plaster; don't overfill. When dry, paint with latex primer.

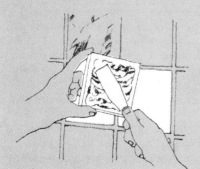

Step 7. When primer dries, apply adhesive to back of new tile with putty knife. Keep adhesive about ½" away from edge of tile.

Step 8. With a hammer and block of wood, gently tap tile in place until level. Hold in place with spacers and tape. Wait 24 hours before grouting.

Step 9. Apply grout with rubber-backed trowel and clean face of tile with damp sponge and dry cloth.

. . . Continued from page 51

the tile is up, locate the studs by following down the wall from the ceiling marks with a level. Screw the bars directly to the studs through holes drilled in the tile.

Setting the Tile

If you want a running bond, center the first tile on the vertical line. Then set the succeeding tiles in the sequence shown, maintaining the step pattern as you cover the wall.

For jack-on-jack bond, set the first tile on the batten with one side aligned exactly with the vertical line. Press the tile firmly into the adhesive. Don't slide it; this will push adhesive into the joints. Set the succeeding tiles in the same manner, following the sequence illustrated. Use a spacer near each end and both sides of

the tile as you work. Just stick the plastic spacer in the joint; the adhesive will hold it. If you don't have the spacers, use some appropriately sized nails. Regularly check the tile alignment with a straightedge rule.

Continue setting the tiles upward and toward the ends, maintaining the pyramid pattern as illustrated. After laying several tiles, bed them in by hammering lightly on a piece of padded plywood large enough to cover several tiles at once. When you reach the ends of each row, cut the tiles to fit (see page 47). For the last course of tile wainscoting, use either bullnose or cap tiles for a finished effect. When tiling to the ceiling, cut the last course to fit, if necessary. Clean off adhesive carefully as you go.

Corners require special attention. The tiles in an inside corner butt against each other. On outside corners, set one column of tile with bullnose tiles to cover the unfinished edges of the tiles on the adjoining wall. Windows without casings may also pose corner problems. If one of your walls contains a window, finish off the sides and sill with bullnose tiles cut to fit. If the window is trimmed, just take the tile to the trim, leaving space for a grout joint.

After the adhesive has set, carefully remove the supports and the spacers. If you used nails, pull them with pliers, twisting as you pull. Now you are ready to set tiles along the bottom of the wall. If the floor was quite off level, you may have to cut some tiles. Mark and cut the tiles to fit as shown in the drawing below. Place the cut end down. Spread adhesive on the bare wall, and then set the tiles in place. Be sure to bed in these tiles.

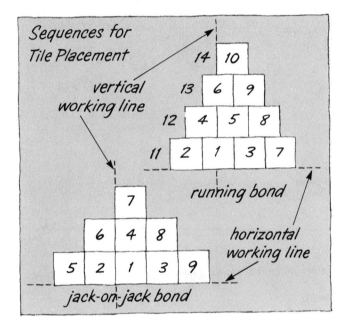

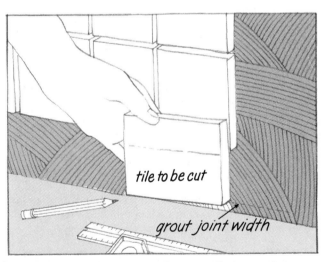

Mark tiles *for the bottom row after removing batten. Be sure to allow for the grout joint at the base.*

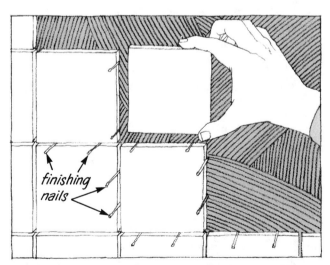

Wall tiles *should be set in step, or pyramid, pattern. Place each with a slight twist; do not slide. Use 6-penny finishing nails to space tiles with no lugs.*

After the adhesive has dried, install any flush-mounted accessories with the same adhesive. Tape these in place while they dry. Clean any adhesive from the face of the tiles and from the grout joints.

The next step is grouting the joints, as described on page 40. Information about grouts and their characteristics begins on page 62.

Tiling a Tub Enclosure

Tiling around a tub is a fairly demanding do-it-yourself project, though it is often a high priority. Especially in older houses, water damage, deteriorated backing, and outdated color schemes are frequent reasons for remodeling. A newly tiled shower or tub enclosure can be a particularly worthwhile and rewarding project.

Preparation

First, cover the drain and line your tub with cardboard to prevent damage. Dropping even a small tool may chip the enamel finish. Remove such fixtures as soap dishes, towel racks, and grab bars. Measure precisely where these items were screwed in, especially the grab bar, so they can be readily reinstalled on the wall studs. Remove handles and escutcheons from the faucets. Wrap masking tape around exposed threads to protect them.

Wet areas such as those around a tub require extra care. The project will take quite a bit of time, so do a thorough job of surface preparation. Replace the backing if needed. Your efforts now will pay off in a tile job that will be functional and beautiful for years.

Study the section on new and existing backings beginning on page 43 and the drawings at the bottom of page 58. If your tub area is already tiled, check it carefully. Is the grout loose or cracked? If so, water has probably weakened the bond and the backing. If there are loose tiles, pull them off and examine the backing. Even if a tile is only slightly loose, pull it off. You don't want your new tile job ruined by the old. If no water damage is present, glue the tiles back in place with an epoxy adhesive. Then clean and prepare all the surfaces to be covered with tile, as described on page 43.

Traditionally, bathroom tile was set in cement mortar because it is waterproof. But today's adhesives and grout are greatly improved and many are also waterproof.

Marking the Working Lines

Accurate, carefully established working lines will help you do professional-looking work on your completed enclosure. Without accurate lines, the rows will not be level and the tiles in the columns will not line up.

The horizontal working line. This line establishes a level line of tile. There are two ways to do it, one if the tub is level and one if it is not (see drawing at right).

Use a level to find the high point of the tub. With level and straightedge, compare the difference at the lower end. If a tub is level to within ⅛", most professionals locate the horizontal working line from the high point. This method uses only full tiles in the bottom row. The slight variation in the gap between the tiles and the out-of-level tub is not noticeable when the gap is caulked.

To establish the horizontal line from the high point of the tub, measure up the width of one tile plus the ⅛" discrepancy in heights plus two grout joint widths (one above and one below the first row). Mark this point.

Then, with your level and a straightedge, extend this line carefully around the enclosure walls. If the adjoining walls are also to be tiled, extend the horizontal working line to them.

If the tub is not level to within ⅛", locate the horizontal line from the low point; otherwise the gap between the top and the bottom of the tiles will be excessive. Then proceed as explained above. Note that you'll have to cut the bottom row of tiles to fit.

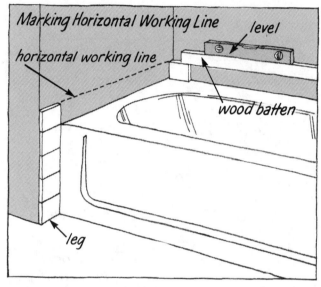

Mark horizontal working line *on back wall at one tile plus ⅛" and 2 grout joint widths up from tub lip. Extend to end walls.*

The vertical working lines. These lines can also be located in more than one way. This is particularly true on the walls at the ends of the tub, where the area to be tiled may vary.

The back wall is where you start in setting tile around a tub. The most pleasing effect is to center the tiles so that those at each end are of equal width. To do this, measure and mark the midpoint of the wall on the horizontal working line. Starting with the edge of one tile on the center mark, stand a row of loose tiles along the back of the tub to determine the size of the end tiles. Don't forget the spacers. If the end tiles are larger than half a tile, work from a centered vertical working line. With level and straightedge, mark the vertical working line on the backing.

If the end tile size is less than half a tile, mark the vertical working line exactly one-half tile to one side or the other of the midpoint. This adjustment avoids narrow end tiles, which are harder to cut and less attractive than larger ones.

If you established your horizontal working line from the low point of the tub, temporarily nail 1" by 3" battens to the wall with the top edges on the horizontal

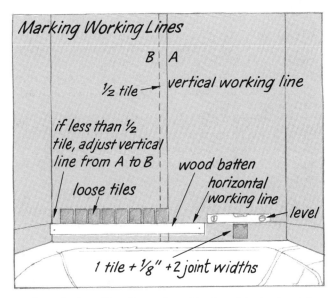

Marking Working Lines

B | A
½ tile → vertical working line
if less than ½ tile, adjust vertical line from A to B
loose tiles
wood batten
horizontal working line
level
1 tile + ⅛" + 2 joint widths

Mark vertical working line *at the midpoint of the horizontal working line.*

working line. Not only do these battens align your tiles, but they prevent them from slipping until the adhesive sets. You can also use the batten method if you're working from the high point of the tub.

The positions of any flush-mounted or recessed accessories, such as soap dishes and towel bars, should be marked on the wall before the adhesive is applied. Don't cover the marks with adhesive. If your accessories were made by the same manufacturer as your tiles, the spaces needed will usually be the same as one or two

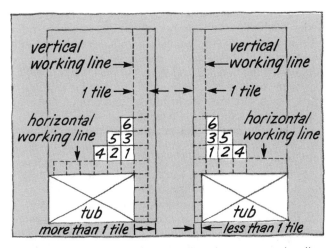

vertical working line →
← vertical working line
1 tile → ← → ← 1 tile
horizontal working line ↓
6
5 3
4 2 1
6
3 5
1 2 4
horizontal working line ↓
tub
more than 1 tile ↦
tub
← less than 1 tile

Typical positions *of the vertical working line on an end wall are shown here.*

tiles. As you set the tiles, just omit tiles wherever the accessories are to go. If you must cut tiles to fit around an object like a soap dish, cut a piece of cardboard the same size and tack it to the wall. Some recessed soap dishes require openings in the backing. If so, tile up to that point, mark the outline on the backing, and cut through the backing.

The end walls are usually laid out after the back wall is covered with tile. On end walls, full tiles should be used on the outer edges, particularly if tile extends to the floor beside the tub. Position your vertical working line to minimize the number of cut tiles and locate them in a corner.

The illustration below shows typical positions of the vertical working line on an end wall. Choose the one that best suits your situation; then make a dry run with loose tiles to check the layout for inconvenient cuts. Cut tiles should go down the inside corners. Sometimes a minor adjustment in the position of the vertical line can make your work easier. When you're satisfied, mark the vertical lines on both end walls. If your situation is unusual, consult your tile dealer, distributor, or manufacturer.

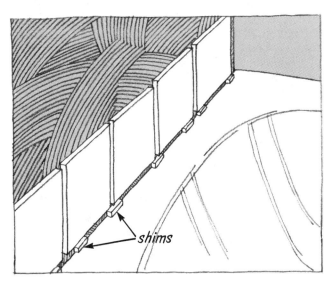

shims

For level tub, *place shims between tiles and tub to align tile tops with horizontal working line.*

Some final hints. Before you go on to the next step and spread the adhesive, mark another horizontal line where your tiles will end (unless you're going to the ceiling). This top horizontal line will guide you as you apply the adhesive so you won't spread more than necessary. With a tile stick (see page 48), mark the top of the last tile row on the vertical lines. You should have at least one row above the shower head. Once you have marked the points on the vertical working lines, extend a horizontal line through them around the tub enclosure.

Laying the Tile

At last you're ready to start laying tiles. When installing square or rectangular tiles, you have a choice of two patterns. Jack-on-jack has all its joints aligned and is traditional in bathrooms. In a running bond the joints are staggered, which involves more tile cutting. Both are illustrated on page 53.

The method for setting the more common jack-on-jack bond is described in the following discussion. To set the running bond, place the middle of the first tile on your vertical working line. Then set the succeeding tiles in the sequence illustrated on page 53.

Tiling the back wall. Spread your adhesive on the back wall as described on page 46. Be sure to leave blank spaces in the marked locations for later installation of accessories.

Setting the first tile. If you nailed a batten support to the wall, set the first tile at the intersection of the vertical guideline and the batten (see page 53, top). Set the tile firmly but don't slide it. Make sure that the tile is tight against the batten with one edge aligned exactly with the vertical line.

When working without a batten, you should still set the first tile at the intersection of the two working lines, but the top edge is aligned with the horizontal working line. Use spacers or wood shims between the tub and the bottom of the tiles to keep them from sliding. Press firmly to bed the tile in the bond coat.

Building the pyramid. Now set a tile on each side of the first tile, with the bottoms on the batten. Use spacers or, if the tiles have built-in spacing lugs, make sure they are tight against each other. Set each tile firmly. If one edge or corner rides up, use your trowel handle to tap until flush with the adjoining tile.

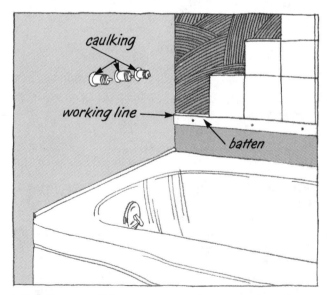

Install tiles *on wall in step, or pyramid, pattern. After adhesive dries, remove batten and place tiles in remaining space.*

Set the next tile—the fourth—in the same fashion, exactly above the first one, with one edge on the vertical working line. Continue setting tiles in the sequence shown on page 53, adding spacers as needed. As the pyramid develops in a step pattern, make sure that the corners are aligned and check the joints. Painstaking attention to detail will ensure a professional-looking job.

As you reach the ends of each row, measure, mark, and cut the end tiles as needed (see box on "Marking and Cutting Ceramic Tiles," page 47). Check your rows with a batten and level and adjust any tile that may have slipped.

Finishing the top. If you are tiling only part way up the wall, the last course or row of tiles should be bull-nose tiles. These have one edge rounded and glazed; they may be full-size or half-size tiles (sometimes known as caps).

If you are tiling all the way to the ceiling, you'll probably have to cut the last row to fit. Measure, mark, and cut these tiles and set them as you go along.

After setting the last tile, check your work. Are all the joints aligned? If not, wiggle the offending tiles into position. If any tiles project above their neighbors, bed them in again with a mallet or hammer and block of padded wood.

Clean any adhesive from the face of the tile and from the joints if filled with adhesive.

Tiling the end walls. Now that you have finished the back wall, the end walls are next. Spread adhesive on the wall opposite the shower head; it's the easier of the two.

If you're laying tile in a running bond, you may want to adjust your starting point. Corner tiles of equal width on the adjoining walls give a more pleasing appearance. Check by making a dry run. In any event, stagger alternate rows by half the width of a tile, as you did on the back wall.

Place the first tile at the intersection of the vertical working line and the batten. Make sure that the tile is tight against the batten and that one edge is exactly on the vertical line.

If you're working without a batten, align the top edge of the tile with the horizontal working line and insert shims between the tile's bottom edge and the tub lip to prevent slipping.

Place the second and third tiles as shown in the drawing on page 55, bottom, aligning them with the first. Make sure they are firmly set, and don't forget the spacers if your tiles don't have lugs.

Continue setting tiles, maintaining the step pattern as you work toward the corner. Bed the tiles in as you go, and check alignment frequently. In the corner, cut tiles to fit as needed. If you're not tiling to the ceiling, set the top row with bullnose tiles to finish it off.

Next spread your adhesive on the other wall and lay the tiles in a similar manner. This wall requires more effort because you must cut tiles to fit around the faucet and shower head pipes (see below and the box "Marking and Cutting Ceramic Tiles," on page 47).

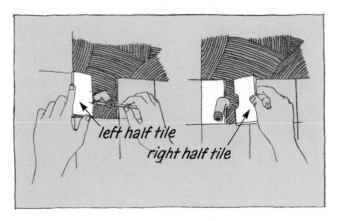

Mark pipe center *on tile's top edge and cut in two. Then mark pipe on cut edge of each piece (left). Remove excess with nippers and set pieces in place (right).*

Install accessories, *such as soap dish, last. Apply adhesive either to wall or to back of accessory. Tape them in place until adhesive dries.*

While waiting for the adhesive to set, check your work and realign any tiles that need it. Carefully clean off any adhesive from the faces of the tile and clean out the joints if needed.

After the adhesive has set, carefully remove the battens. Spread adhesive between the bottom of the tile and the tub lip. Set tiles in the vacant space, cutting them to fit if necessary. When cutting, maintain the grout space between tiles and tub. Don't forget to bed these tiles in.

Now set the legs (the tiles in front of the tub on either side) and the columns of tiles above them. Depending on your situation, these may be bullnose tiles, field tiles, or a combination of both.

If your towel bars, soap dish, and other accessories are also ceramic, and if they are flush-mounted or recessed, now is the time to set them. Tape them in place until the adhesive dries. Metal accessories shouldn't be set until you have grouted the joints. Some manufacturers say to set the accessory with grout—but don't. Use epoxy; it's waterproof.

Finishing Up

While you're waiting for the adhesive to dry, clean excess adhesive from the tile faces and the joints. Grout the joints as described in "Mixing and Applying Grout," on page 62.

With a good bathtub caulk, seal the opening between the bottom of the tiles and the tub. But before you begin be sure that both the tiles and grout are dry. Wait at least two weeks—this will give the grout a chance to cure completely.

Use the same caulk for the openings between the tiles and the faucets and shower head. If you're using surface-mounted accessories, mark and drill the holes and fasten the accessories with toggle bolts or other type of anchor. Soap dishes require a bead of caulking applied behind the flange. Wipe off any that squeezes out when you mount the dish.

After the grout has dried and you've sealed it (see page 63), your tub is ready to use.

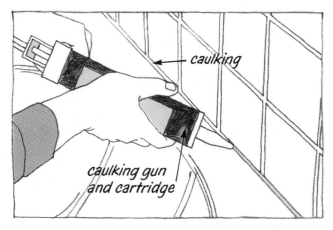

Filling gap *between tile and tub or shower with caulk seals backing and adhesive from water.*

Thoroughly seal openings *between pipes and tile with good-quality bathtub caulk.*

Tiling a Shower

The wet and steamy environment of a shower demands careful attention to selection and installation of the backing, choice of adhesive, and installation of the tile. Care must be taken to grout the tile and seal around accessories. The restricted working space in many showers adds to the difficulty.

Traditionally the shower pan, or the bottom of the shower, was constructed on the job with cement mortar, a waterproof membrane, and ceramic tile. This is best left to a professional. A variety of prefabricated shower pans are available for those who wish to build their own showers.

Tiling a shower is similar to tiling a tub enclosure, so the instructions beginning on page 54 will help you. The shower pan has the same relationship to the tile as a tub does.

Preparation

If you are remodeling and the shower area is backed with regular gypsum wallboard, tear it out and install water-resistant wallboard or cement backer board. Use the same material on the ceiling. If at all possible, install a ceiling vent.

Laying Out the Job

As with a tub enclosure, mark the working lines first on the back wall and then on the sides. If your shower walls partially enclose the front, use the back corners as your vertical working lines if the back wall is plumb. Any cut tiles will be hidden in the front corners.

Setting the Tile

Spread adhesive on the back wall and set the tiles as described in "Tiling a Tub Enclosure," page 54. When

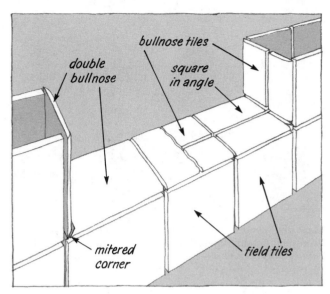

Two ways to trim *a shower opening: right half shows opening trimmed with bullnose caps; left half has double bullnose tiles. Slope bottom of opening slightly toward inside of shower.*

the back is complete, do the sides of the shower. Tile work on the front of an enclosed shower is done last. Set any ceramic accessories after the adhesive has dried and support them with tape while the adhesive sets.

If you want to tile your ceiling, do it before the walls. Support the tile with strips of plywood over each course supported by lengths of 2 by 4s wedged between pan and ceiling.

Grouting & Finishing Up

After the adhesive is dry, carefully grout all the joints between the tiles (see page 62). Use a good bathtub caulk to seal the joints between shower pan and tile and around faucet handles, shower head, and the soap dish or other accessories. After the grout has dried, apply a sealer as described on page 63.

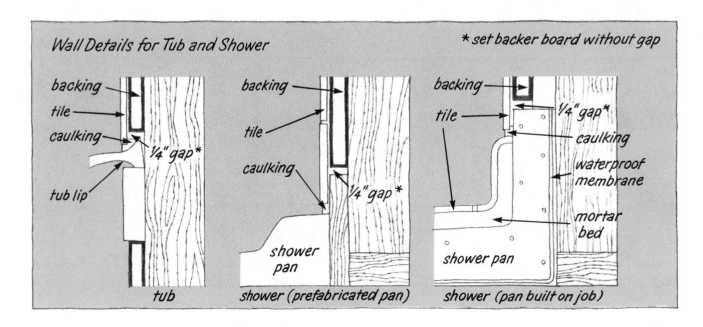

Tiling Sinks & Countertops

Installing ceramic tile on a countertop or similar surface is a good project for the beginner. A sink top in the bathroom or kitchen, a new top for a bar or vanity, an elegant buffet in the dining room, or open storage shelves in the kitchen are all reasonably easy projects that can bring major changes to a room.

The following instructions, which explain how to tile a sink top, can be adapted to other projects. If you are tiling a countertop or buffet, just ignore the portion about sinks. If you want to tile storage shelves, forget the sinks and backsplashes.

Choosing the edge trim. Before you start, decide how you'll trim the counter edge. The usual methods are illustrated below; your choice will depend on the availability of trim pieces in your pattern as well as on personal preference. The trim is commonly one-piece rounded cap trim, also called sink cap or sinkrail. Edge trim can also be two pieces of tile, with the top piece overlapping the tile on the edge.

If you're using quarter-round tiles for trim, you can either miter the corners or use the quarter-round corner trim available in some patterns.

Selecting a sink. The type of sink influences your project. There are two basic types: recessed, which means the sink is slightly lower than the counter tile, and self-rimming, which means it sits on top of the tile. Self-rimming sinks are much easier for tiling projects because you tile up to the opening cut in the counter and then just drop your sink in place on a line of caulk. Recessed sinks require careful cutting of numerous trim pieces around the edge between counter tile and sink.

Preparation

You can apply new tiles right over existing ceramic tile or laminated plastic counters. Refer to the section on existing backings, page 44, for information on preparing these surfaces. That section also tells you how to pre-pare the wall before installing a tile backsplash. The wall covering is generally gypsum wallboard.

If you installed new cabinets or removed the old countertop, you'll be installing a new backing for the counter. By far the most common backing for ceramic tile countertops is ¾" exterior grade plywood. If you are installing a recessed sink, it's best to cover the plywood with cement backer board because there is increased risk of water penetration around the sink. Backer board cannot be used flat without plywood support.

Make sure the plywood countertop is rigid and well supported. If the width of the top is 24" or less, a cross-brace every 36" is adequate. Where plywood pieces are butted together at the ends, leave about ⅛" space to permit expansion. Similarly, there should be about ⅛" gap between the plywood and the back wall. A wood batten placed underneath temporarily will prevent the adhesive from dripping into the cabinets.

The illustrations below show methods for trimming along edges and around sinks. Be sure to leave enough clearance between the edge trim and appliances that pull out, such as a dishwasher. Any overhangs must be firmly braced; a length of 1" by 2" or 2" by 2" can be screwed under the edge as backing for the edge trim.

With a plywood backing, you may use either a high quality water-resistant mastic or an epoxy adhesive. With cement backer board, both thin-set and epoxy adhesive are commonly used; epoxy is often preferred on plywood around sink areas because it's waterproof. For added protection, many manufacturers recommend sealing the face and edges of the plywood.

Planning the Layout

If you're installing a sink in a plywood countertop, mark its center point on the front edge of the plywood. If your countertop won't have a sink, mark the midpoint of the top. In either case the point you mark will be a reference point for starting your tile work.

Make a dry run with edge and field tiles along the counter, all properly spaced and aligned. If there is a corner on the cabinet, the edge of a full tile must be in line with the corner. Adjust the tile from the sink while trying to maintain more than half a tile at the sink's

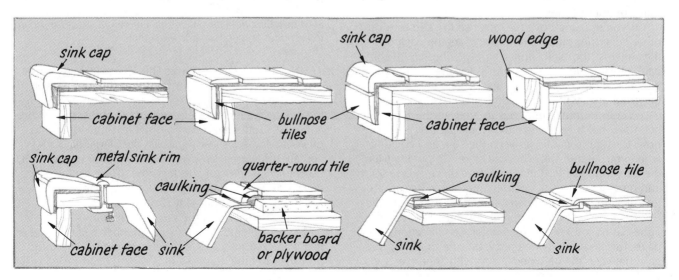

edge. Cut the final pieces that fit against the wall. If your layout doesn't seem to fit, try adjusting it with one or more rows of half tiles.

By resolving any problems before you start setting the tiles, you'll improve the look of the finished job. You can mark and cut the tiles now or wait until you are ready to set them. It's important that you allow for the cove tiles along the back if you are using them for the backsplash.

After arriving at the optimum layout, you may feel that you'll have difficulty duplicating it when you set the tiles. If this is the case, either mark the locations of key tiles on the backing or set the edge trim before you remove the other tiles (see "Setting the Tile," below). Then you can mark your reference points on the edge trim.

Setting the Tile

Set the edge trim before you spread the adhesive for the field tiles. The field tiles are generally in line with the edge trim.

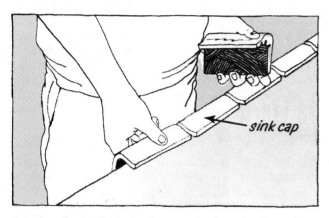

Set edge tiles *in place after buttering backs with adhesive.*

If your edge trim consists of two pieces (see page 59) instead of the one-piece sink cap, set the vertical piece on the front of the counter first. Tape these in place until the adhesive sets.

If you're using cove tile, after all the cap trim or other edge trim pieces are in place, set the back cove tiles against the wall. Butter (apply adhesive to) the back of each tile and press firmly and evenly into place. Be sure to line the cove tiles up with the edge tiles so the grout lines will run straight between the two.

A self-rimming sink goes in after all the tile has been set, but a recessed sink should be put in place now. Be sure to caulk between the sink and backing when you set the sink. The next step is to put the trim tile around the sink. Butter each trim piece as you set it and press it firmly but carefully into place. Be sure to line tiles up with your reference marks for the field tiles.

After all the trim pieces are positioned, spread the adhesive over a section of counter (see directions on page 46). If you're using epoxy, be sure to fill the ¼" gaps between the plywood sheets with adhesive.

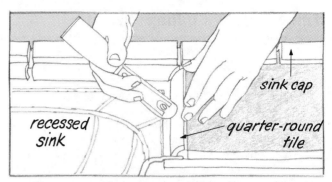

Finish corners *of quarter-round sink trim with round in-angle or by mitering as shown.*

Now lay the field tiles, working from the front to the back and cutting back pieces to fit as necessary. If you're not using a back cove, the tiles should run to the wall. Work from the sink toward the ends so you'll have full tiles around the sink. Small cut tiles around the sink are an invitation to leakage. If your project has no sink, start laying the field tiles from the center of the counter and work toward the ends. Both ends should have tiles of equal size. Be sure to use spacers if the tiles don't have lugs (see page 46). Check the grout joint alignment frequently. Use a piece of padded plywood large enough to cover several squares at once and tap with a mallet or hammer to bed and level the tile faces as you lay them.

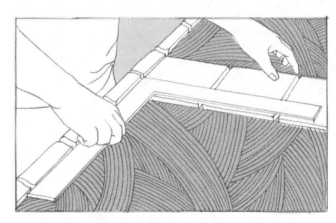

Start installing *field tiles by setting column of tiles. Use square to keep tiles perpendicular to edge trim.*

Now set the backsplash. This is an ideal area to set some handpainted tiles to highlight the area. If you used cove tiles, continue setting the tiles on the wall to the height desired after covering most of the area with adhesive. Butter the last row of tiles individually to prevent adhesive showing above the tiled area. Unless you are tiling up to an overhead cabinet or window sill, use bullnose tiles for the last row. If you didn't use cove tiles, start the backsplash with regular field tiles. Space them one grout width above the counter tiles.

If the wall behind the counter contains electrical outlets or switches, you can stop the backsplash short of them, tile partially around them, or cut the tile to fit over the opening. Rarely will a tile fall dead center over

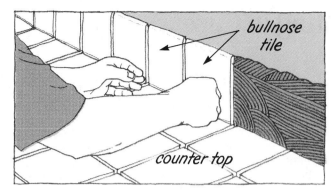

Align joints of backsplash tiles with joints on countertop. Leave width of one grout joint between counter tiles and bottom of backsplash tiles.

When backsplash is higher than one course, you may have to fit tiles around electrical outlets. Either cut hole in tile or cut tile in two and nibble out hole.

an opening, so you probably will have to cut to bring the face out flush with the tile, as described on page 53.

A window sill behind a sink can be finished with bullnose tiles or the tile can run up to the sill. Some faucets are mounted on the wall behind the sink. If this is your situation, mark and cut the tiles to fit around the pipes as described on page 47.

Applying Grout

Clean any adhesive that might have stuck to the tile faces. After the adhesive has dried for the prescribed time, grout the tiles as described on page 62. If you're using cement-base grout, when it's thoroughly dry be sure to seal it (see "Caring for Ceramic Tile," page 63).

Some Quick & Simple Projects

If you've never installed ceramic tile, you may want to begin with a small project that will improve your skills and give you quick results. Any of the following projects will add a colorful accent to a room. Because these installations cover small areas, you can use some of the more expensive decorative tiles without straining the budget.

Whether you're tiling a window sill or an entire floor, the basic procedures are the same. Be sure to read the section "How to Prepare the Surface" (see page 42) as well as the information on adhesives and grouts (see pages 39 and 40). To learn the techniques of setting, cutting, and finishing tile, see "How to Install Ceramic Tile (page 46).

Stair treads and risers. Some manufacturers offer a special tile known as step nosing for use on treads. If these are not available, you can use bullnose tiles set with the rounded edges toward the front of the step. A special trim piece called down-corner (see page 35) is ideal for finishing the corners of exposed treads. Use the same installation procedure you would for other horizontal surfaces, such as floors or counters (see pages 48 and 59).

Cover stair risers with field tiles, using the same method you would to tile a wall (see page 51). The top edges of the riser tiles will be covered by the tread nosing.

If you plan to tile both the treads and the risers, do the risers first.

Window sills. Special tiles called window sills are available from some tile makers. Or you can use bullnose tiles; set them with the rounded edges to the front. If the wall below the window is also tiled, the tiles on the sill should overlap the top edges of the wall tiles.

Fireplaces. Tiling the face of a fireplace is similar to installing tile on a wall (see page 51). You can also install a row of the tiles around the inside of the fireplace. Depending on the design of your fireplace, you can use bullnose, double bullnose, or regular field tiles for either job.

If the front of the fireplace is masonry, install the tile with cement-base adhesive. On nonmasonry surfaces, use mastic or epoxy to set the tiles; be sure to let the mastic dry thoroughly—at least 24 hours—before using the fireplace. Tiles installed anywhere inside the fireplace, where they will be directly exposed to the flames, should always be set with cement-base adhesives.

You can tile the hearth just as you would a floor (see page 48). Again, use cement-base adhesives.

Decorative inserts and borders. To add a decorative border of tiles around a door or window, you can fasten tiles directly to the wall with mastic. Use bullnose tiles with the curved edge facing away from the door or window trim.

Another excellent use for a few decorative tiles is to set them in table tops—an end table, a dining room table you might have made, or a picnic table. Not only decorative, they also serve as built-in spots to set hot pans. Lay the tiles in the spacing of your choice, but make sure they are lined up and straight. Mark the edges with a fine-tip pen or pencil. Remove the wood with chisel or router so the tile will be just slightly above the table surface.

To insert tiles in a wall of gypsum board, cut out openings the same size as the tiles. Apply a bead of glue along the edges of a few pieces of wallboard. Slip them at an angle through the opening and fasten against the back side of the wall until dry, closing the opening as much as possible. These pieces will form a recessed backing for the tile.

Final Touches . . . from Grouting to Care

Now you can turn to the finishing touches that will complete your tile project. The first one is applying grout, which fills joints, bonds tiles together, and adds visual appeal. Then comes care of the tile—sealing, waxing, and cleaning.

Grouts

Each type of grout is applied in the same basic way: by first spreading it with a rubber-backed trowel to fill the joints, then removing the excess, cleaning the tile, and allowing it to dry. By contrast, silicone caulking is applied directly to the joints from a tube or cartridge and remains flexible.

Allow the adhesive to set properly before applying grout. Drying time varies with the adhesive, humidity, and temperature, but 24 hours is generally a minimum.

While the adhesive is drying, remove any spacers used to position the tiles. When the adhesive has dried, clean the tile surface so it is completely free of any adhesive. If adhesive is pushed up between some joints, making them too shallow to hold grout, scrape them out. A shallow grout joint will probably crack.

When using a cement-base grout with soft-bodied clay tiles, which are more porous, it is advisable to use a latex additive in the grout. This not only makes it spread more easily but also prevents premature drying of the grout, because some moisture will be drawn into the tiles.

When using epoxy grout for an outdoor patio, keep the grout damp for several days or cover with plastic sheeting so it will cure slowly, which gives it greater strength.

Ideally, grout should be just below the tile surface, to show the tile in relief. If the grout is too low, it is difficult to sponge clean and crumbs and dirt will collect.

Mixing and Applying Grout

Properly mixed cement-base grouts, which require adding water or latex additive to the dry mix, should have the consistency of a pancake batter, neither too stiff nor too soupy. Epoxy grouts should be mixed according to the manufacturer's directions, and they will be of a comparable consistency.

Spreading the grout is relatively simple; it's the proper cleanup that requires careful work. The object is to get the tiles clean without disturbing the grout. Keep a large sponge, a supply of clear water, and soft clean cloths available for the cleanup process. Many grouts can irritate the skin; wear rubber gloves.

If you're using pregrouted panels of wall tiles, note that the spaces between the tiles in each panel are grouted with a flexible, water-repellent silicone, urethane, or polyvinyl chloride rubber. The only additional grouting required is between each panel after it is in place. When using colored grout, remember to mask any vulnerable adjacent surfaces.

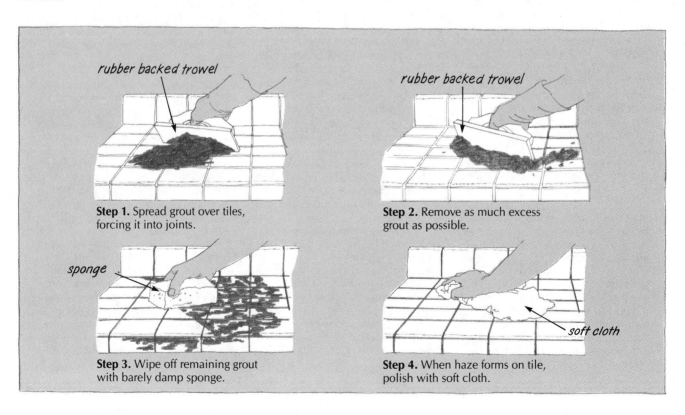

Step 1. Spread grout over tiles, forcing it into joints.

Step 2. Remove as much excess grout as possible.

Step 3. Wipe off remaining grout with barely damp sponge.

Step 4. When haze forms on tile, polish with soft cloth.

These are the steps involved in applying grout.

1) Spread about a cup of grout to familiarize yourself with the process. On counters and floors, just pour some from the bucket; on walls, dip the grout up with your rubber-backed trowel. Hold the leading edge of the trowel up at about a 30° angle and spread the grout firmly over the tile. Work the trowel back and forth at different angles to the grout to force it into the joints. It is important that the joints are filled, with no voids or air pockets.

2) After this first area, perhaps 5 square feet, has been grouted, scrape off the trowel and go over it again to pick up the excess. This time hold the trowel at about a 50° angle and work at a diagonal to the joints to minimize disturbing the grout there. Clean your trowel repeatedly in a bucket of water as you work.

3) Now comes the tricky part. The layer of grout still on the tile must be cleaned off before it dries, but you shouldn't do it too soon. The grout must be in the process of firming up. You don't want to disturb the grout, so this calls for careful work. Wipe the tile with a damp sponge at an angle to the grout lines and rinse the sponge often. If the grout seems too soft, move on to the next area to be grouted and come back a little later. When the tiles are as clean as you can get them, let the grout dry until a haze appears over the surface of the tile.

4) When the grout has hardened, go back and wipe off the haze with soft, clean cloths, again without disturbing the grout in the joints. The tiles must be wiped almost individually. After they are all clean, let the grout dry overnight. If grout has ridden up onto the tile in some spots, use the back of an old toothbrush or a small stick wrapped in a cloth to clean along the tile edges.

Caring for Ceramic Tile

Once you've installed the tile and had a chance to stand back and admire your work, you should take steps to keep the tile looking new for years to come. Unglazed tile and cement-base grouts both need sealers. With newer sealers this only needs to be done once. Glazed tiles and epoxy grouts don't need to be sealed. Beyond that, routine cleaning is all that's needed to keep tile looking good.

Sealing Tile & Grout

Most sealers use silicone or lacquer as a base. Silicone-base sealers are generally used in and around showers, bathtubs, and other wet areas. They wipe off glazed tile surfaces easily and penetrate the cement-base grout between the tiles. Lacquer-base sealers break down in wet areas, but they penetrate unglazed tile pores better than the silicone sealers. You can get lacquer-base sealers in gloss and nongloss finishes. The gloss finish may make tiles slippery, so test the sealer before you apply it to floors.

Follow manufacturer's instructions for applying tile and grout sealers. On new tile installations, wait at least 2 weeks before applying the sealer to give the grout a chance to cure completely. Both tiles and grout should be completely dry. Sealing tile is basically just a matter of spreading it on and wiping off any film. Grout sealer requires more care; you must spread it over tile and grout and then wipe the tile before it hardens. Some grout sealers will put a shine on tile. Although attractive, this can make a bathroom floor slippery. Discuss this with your dealer.

Working with Panels & Mosaics

Panels of wall tile (see page 35) and sheets of mosaic are similar: in both, numerous tiles are mounted on fiberglass mesh. The panels are pregrouted, but the mosaics must be grouted in the standard manner after they are laid.

The basic installation method is the same as that for individual tiles. Instead of handling individual tiles, you use sheets containing 1 or 2 square feet of tile.

The requirements for surface preparation and backings are the same, and you must lay out working lines with panels and sheets as with single tiles.

Sheets and panels are much faster to install than single tiles, so you'll find you can cover larger areas with adhesive. Tiles in a panel are held firmly in position by the grout, but those in a mosaic sheet are not, despite the mesh backing. You may have to move them about slightly right after laying them in the adhesive to keep the grout lines straight. Check frequently for alignment.

The only grouting necessary on pregrouted panels is for the joints between the panels. Use a caulking gun for this. Grouting mosaics is the same as for individual tiles.

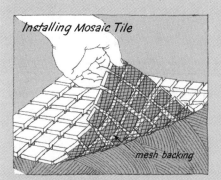

Installing Mosaic Tile

mesh backing

Mosaic tiles *come mounted in sheets.*

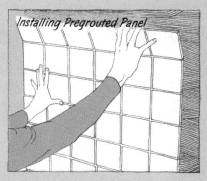

Installing Pregrouted Panel

Pregrouted *tile panels save time.*

Tile Waxes

After they are sealed, unglazed tile floors may be waxed and buffed for additional beauty and protection. Tile waxes should be used only in dry areas because standing water may discolor them.

After cleaning the surface, apply the wax according to label directions and then buff with a floor polisher. A properly applied wax will last several years, requiring only an occasional buffing. Too much wax left on the tile's surface, however, can turn yellow in a few years. If this happens, strip off the old wax by scrubbing with hot water and detergent, or rent a commercial wax stripper.

Cleaning Tips

Ceramic tile is one of the easiest surfaces to keep clean. Routine cleaning requires only washing with hot water and a mild detergent or all-purpose household cleaner. To prevent stains, wipe up spills as soon as they happen.

After washing the tile, rinse it thoroughly to remove detergent film; then wipe dry with a soft, dry cloth. For stubborn dirt, scrub tiles with a white cleansing powder. Don't use a cleaner containing bleach; this can pull the color out of colored grouts.

You might also try a commercial tile cleaner available from your dealer or in hardware stores. Read the directions and precautions on the labels of tile cleaners before using them. Some tile cleaners have harsh acids that will etch glazed tiles if left on the surface too long—use them sparingly. **Never mix cleaners containing acid or ammonia with chlorine bleach. The chemical reaction releases the chlorine as a poisonous gas.**

On floors, use a broom or dust mop for removing loose dirt and a damp mop for cleaning. For other surfaces (walls, countertops, and so on), use a sponge or cloth to apply the cleaning solution. For rough scrubbing, use a stiff-bristled scrub brush or nylon scrubbing pad. Avoid using steel wool pads on ceramic tiles—they may cause rust stains.

In addition to routine cleaning, you can keep grout looking new by scrubbing it occasionally with a toothbrush and a household cleaner that does not contain bleach. If your grout is colored, test these cleaners in an unobtrusive place before you use them. It's hard to predict how the chemicals will react with the pigment in the grout.

If you have hard water, spots and deposits may build up on tiles that are in shower enclosures, on sink counters, and in other wet areas. You can help prevent such buildups by keeping the tile surfaces dry. Use a sponge to wipe water off the tiles after showering or doing dishes. To remove water deposits and soap film from the tile, apply household ammonia or a one-to-one mixture of vinegar and water, rinse thoroughly, and dry.

Removing Stains from Tile

Even the hardest tile surface may pick up a stain or two. Tile, grout, and stains all come in so many kinds that no simple rules for stain removal can be given. The chart below covers the most common and troublesome stains. If a stain remains after one try, try again. If the cleaner you are using seems too weak, make it more concentrated. In most cases, heating a solution will cause it to work faster.

Replacing Grout

If grout is cracked, badly worn, or permanently stained, you can replace it. Scrape the old grout from the joints with a lever-type can opener or narrow-tip screwdriver. Scrub the joint surfaces clean with an old toothbrush and apply the grout as described on page 62. Most hardware stores sell grout in small quantities for replacement purposes.

What to Do When Tiles Get Stained

Stain	Cleaner & Method
Ink, blood, coffee, mustard, fruit juice.	Use a nonbleach cleaner and leave on surface for several minutes; then rinse off.
Motor oil (on quarry or patio tile)	Use fluid mixture of plaster of Paris to draw out stain. Brush over surface, let dry for 24 hours, and scrape off with stiff broom; repeat if necessary.
Vegetable oil (on quarry or patio tile)	Scrub with detergent. If that doesn't work, scrub surface with 10% sodium carbonate (washing soda) solution in water. Mop with 5% sodium hydroxide (caustic soda) for faster action.
Hard water stains, rust marks	Scrub with nonbleach scouring powder; rinse.
Paint (new stain)	Apply commercial paint remover, let stand, and then scrape off loose paint with razor blade.
Paint (old stain), dried plaster	Scrape loose paint or plaster off with razor blade; finish with paint remover.

Some Other Choices in Tile Materials

In addition to the popular tiles—ceramic, wood, and resilient—covered in this book, you'll also find tiles made from other materials. Perhaps one of the kinds discussed below will be just right for your remodeling job.

Carpet tiles are easily installed over most smooth floor surfaces. Most commonly available in 12" squares, these tiles have a built-in foam padding. Carpet tiles come in three kinds: those with a self-stick backing; those with a nonskid rubber backing that requires no adhesive; and those laid with an adhesive in the same way as resilient tiles. Carpet tiles are easy to replace if they become worn or damaged.

Mirror tiles, usually 12" square, come with a wide variety of surface designs. Applied to a wall, they add depth and light to any room. They are affixed to a surface with double-faced mounting tape.

Marble tiles, precut to various sizes, may be used in the same ways as ceramic tile. Long considered a hallmark of opulence, marble tiles cost about the same as high-quality ceramic tiles or hardwood flooring. Installation is similar to that of cermaic tile.

Slate tiles are bluish black, green, or maroon in color, with either a smooth or—more often—a textured surface. Slate floors are durable and restful to the eyes.

Terrazzo tile is made by setting chips of marble or onyx in concrete and polishing the surface. Though commonly made in large slabs, terrazzo is also available in 12" tiles that can be installed by the homeowner.

Polyester tiles (sometimes called epoxy tiles) consist of pulverized stone bonded in polyester or other plastic. These extremely durable tiles are set like ceramic tile.

Metal tiles of copper, stainless steel, or aluminum harmonize well with kitchen appliances. Metal tiles are easy to clean and won't chip or crack.

Plastic tiles can replace ceramic tiles in low-wear, high-moisture situations such as tub and shower enclosures. They cost about one-fifth as much as their ceramic equivalents.

Marble *is just one of many other kinds of tiling materials available; installation is similar to ceramic tile. Tile by Bufalini Marble Corporation.*

Resilient Tile

... attractive, economical, easy to maintain

Traditional or contemporary, *simulated brick or marble, textured or smooth, resilient tile offers a wide variety of look-alikes as well as original designs.*

Does a new floor with the appearance of Italian marble or Spanish tile appeal to you? How about one with a wild, colorful graphic design or the look of elegant slate? From traditional to contemporary, today's resilient tiles offer a vast range of colors, textures, and patterns to whet your creative appetite. These individual tiles, usually 9″ by 9″ or 12″ by 12″, are commonly made of a vinyl composition or solid vinyl. Resilient tiles can simulate almost every known flooring material but also offer many of their own unique designs.

Compared to many other floorings, resilient tiles are economical and easy to install and maintain. Installation requires only some basic skills, patience, and a few simple tools. Resilient tiles are also suitable for walls; however, they are not recommended for countertops because they're easily damaged by sharp objects.

Resilient tiles are more commonly used by commercial firms than by homeowners, who generally use less expensive sheet vinyl. But consider that if one or two tiles are damaged, they can be replaced. Damaged sheet vinyl can mean redoing the whole floor.

About Resilient Tile

When you shop for resilient tile, you'll find a startling selection of designs, colors, textures, and new materials. A few years ago resilient tiles were made of asphalt or vinyl-asbestos. Now they're made almost exclusively of solid vinyl or vinyl composition.

Making your Choice

Vinyl tiles. Vinyl composition and solid vinyl tiles dominate the market in resilient tiles. They are virtually waterproof and highly resistant to wear, dirt, and indentation. They can be put down with adhesives, and they also come in a self-stick variety: just peel off the paper backing and stick the tile to the floor. Most of these resilient tiles come with a no-wax finish to make cleaning easy.

Variations. Some variations of vinyl tiles involve materials such as fabric, hardwood veneers, or marble chips. These materials are suspended in solid vinyl or laminated between a base and a tough vinyl surface. Resilient tiles designed especially for walls include simulated

brick, wood shake, and ceramic designs. You can even buy a special grout to give simulated ceramic and brick designs a more realistic look.

Asphalt tile. The forerunner of modern resilient tiles, asphalt tile is still available for replacement purposes, though it is increasingly hard to find. Less durable than solid vinyl tiles and available in fewer patterns and colors, asphalt tile is rarely installed in homes today.

Vinyl-asbestos tile. This longer-lasting and more colorful tile replaced asphalt tile in popularity until studies showed asbestos to be a health hazard. This material is no longer on the market. If you think it might be in your house, do *not* tear it up or sand it. Simply cover with another flooring material.

Other Considerations

Once you have decided on resilient tile, you'll want to choose a design, color, and texture to complement your room decor. Here are a few points to consider while making your choice.

Ask whether the tile has the color and pattern printed on it or whether it is inlaid, meaning it is continuous to the tile backing. Inlaid tile is more expensive but the color and pattern will not wear off.

Vinyl composition tiles are less likely to scratch than solid vinyl tiles.

Embossed tiles are finished with a grained or fissured surface. Embossing helps hide wear marks and indentations left by furniture, but deeply embossed tiles can collect dirt.

Solid colors, especially black and white, tend to show dirt more than marbled or patterned tiles.

Hold different tiles to the light to compare the quality of the color and the depth it appears to have.

Ask if a warranty comes with the tile. Some offer lifetime warranties against the color or pattern wearing off.

How Much Will You Need?

Resilient tiles come in two standard sizes, 9″ square and 12″ square. Other sizes and shapes are available, but they often must be ordered specially.

To find the amount of tile you need, first find the area of the floor by multiplying the overall length of the

Feature strips *set off plain tile designs.*

Create floor design *on graph paper with colored pencils.*

room by its width, both in feet. Deduct the area of any protrusions into the room, such as a kitchen counter or a bathtub. For a room with an odd shape, such as an L-shaped room, divide the floor area into rectangles. Then measure each and add the areas together. Once you have found the area, add 5 percent so you will have extra tiles for cutting, waste, and later repairs.

Resilient tile comes in boxes that contain enough to cover 45 square feet. To find the number of boxes you need, divide the overall floor area (including the 5 percent extra) by 45. Unless tiles must be ordered specially, most tile dealers will break a box to sell you the exact number of tiles you want. Check boxes for color consistency.

If your design uses more than one color or pattern, you can estimate how many tiles of each kind you will need by drawing your design on graph paper with colored pencils.

When you buy the tile, discuss with the dealer the type you want and the surface on which you plan to put it. At the same time, select an adhesive compatible with the backing (unless using self-stick tiles). Choose the correct notched trowel to spread it, unless the manufacturer suggests that the adhesive be rolled on. Your tile dealer will help you choose these items.

Refer to the section on preparing the surface, on the facing page, to determine if you'll need additional tools and materials for preliminary work.

Tools You'll Need

You may already have most of the tools needed to install resilient tile. To measure and mark the working lines, you'll need a steel tape measure, square, pencil, and chalk line. If you'll be marking lines on walls, you'll also need a level.

To cut the tiles in straight lines, use a utility knife and square to guide the cut. Curves or angles can be cut with a pair of heavy scissors.

To spread the adhesive, you'll need a brush, paint roller, or notched trowel—whichever is specified by

the tile or adhesive manufacturer. And to bed vinyl tiles firmly it is best to use a 150-pound floor roller, although you can press a section of the floor with a rolling pin.

How to Install Resilient Tile

The key to a professional-looking job is proper planning and careful work. Resilient tiles don't require grout, but are laid tightly against each other. Often a simulated or even recessed grout line is part of the pattern. But because these tiles are made with machine precision, unlike some of the more rugged-looking ceramic floor tiles, they must be laid out in perfectly straight lines.

You need a suitable subfloor (discussed below) on which to lay the tile. You must lay out accurate working lines so tiles along opposite walls will be of comparable size. Finally, you must ensure that the tiles adhere tightly and smoothly to the subfloor. Follow the methods outlined in this section as well as any instructions provided with the tile you're installing.

Before you start, remove from the floor everything that isn't nailed down—and some things that are. This includes base molding, thresholds (if any), and doors that swing into the room. If the base molding has a shoe—usually a length of quarter-round molding along the lower edge—only the shoe needs to be removed. If you plan to put the same base or shoe molding back after you finish tiling, pry it carefully from the wall with a wood chisel, remove the nails, and patch the nail holes in each strip. If your plans call for replacing the wood base molding with vinyl cove molding, be careful not to damage the walls as you remove the wood base.

Preparing the Surface

Resilient tile can be installed over almost any existing surface if the surface is properly prepared. Generally, the surface must be structurally sound, dry, and free from foreign matter such as grease, wax, dirt, and old finish. You can lay resilient tile over floors painted with latex if the paint is in good condition—no peeling, flaking, or chalking.

General directions for preparing common floor surfaces for resilient tile are given below. Follow these in conjunction with the directions that come with the tile you're installing.

Old resilient floors. Resilient tile can be installed over an existing resilient floor if the existing floor is smooth (not embossed or textured) and still sticks tightly to the subfloor. But all old wax must be removed before the new floor is laid. Your dealer has compounds for cleaning the floor. If your floor doesn't meet these requirements, you must either remove the existing flooring or cover it with a new backing, generally ¼" exterior plywood. Vinyl floors laid with epoxy adhesives are difficult to remove; these are also best covered with plywood sheets. **Caution: Do not sand or tear up the floor if it is vinyl-asbestos. This material contains fibers that can damage your lungs if inhaled. If in doubt, just cover the floor with ¼" plywood.**

To remove resilient sheet flooring, cut it into strips about 6" wide with a utility knife or linoleum knife, being careful not to damage the subfloor. The flooring will come up rather easily as it separates from the backing, which is still stuck to the floor. Soak this backing in water—without flooding the floor—and then use a floor scraper to remove it. When the exposed subfloor is dry, fill any low spots or holes with a trowel-on patching material recommended by the tile manufacturer.

To remove old resilient tiles, use a floor scraper as shown in the drawing below. If tiles don't come up easily, warm them to soften the adhesive. You can do this with an old iron or a propane torch. (Heating won't

help with epoxy adhesives.) Once you break the tiles loose you'll find the floor still covered with the rough adhesive. Paint on adhesive remover, allow to stand, then scrape up the softened adhesive. If you can't remove the tiles, cover with an underlayment sheet.

Wood floors. If you are planning to lay resilient tile over wood subfloors or wood-finish floors, they must be smooth and flat. A subfloor of 1" by 4" tongue-and-groove, common in older homes, should be covered with a ½" plywood underlayment because it is probably too springy for tile. An old and rough-finished wood floor can be smoothed with a floor sander unless there are nails on the surface, in which case it is easier to cover with plywood than to set all the nails.

If your house has no basement, only a tight crawl-space under the floors, there is a risk of dampness from the ground working its way into the house. A house with wood floors over a crawlspace should be protected by plastic sheeting placed on the ground under the house to form a vapor barrier. Without this, moisture can cause the wood to swell and buckle. Put the vapor barrier down and make sure the wood floors are dry before you lay new tile.

Plywood underlayment often may have cracks and indentations where knots have fallen out. Fill these with a hard-drying wood filler and smooth with a trowel. Put the plywood down with 1½"-long 4-penny ring-shank nails spaced every 6" along the edges and 12" in the field (down the middle portion where the floor joists would be). Leave gaps about ¹⁄₃₂" between the sheets and ⅛" along the walls to permit expansion.

Another reminder: don't use particleboard as an underlayment for resilient tile. It disintegrates if it gets wet and ruins your floor. It is, however, commonly used under sheet vinyl floors, which are waterproof.

Floor scraper quickly removes large sections of old resilient tile or resilient sheet flooring.

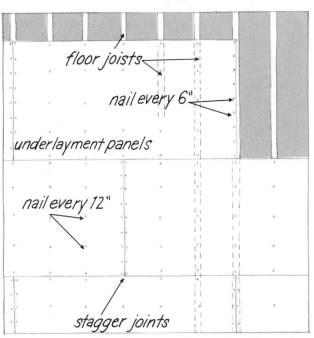

floor joists

nail every 6"

underlayment panels

nail every 12"

stagger joints

Stagger joints *on plywood underlayment panels. Offset nails around edges. Set nail heads slightly below surface; fill holes, joints with patching material.*

Concrete floors. If resilient tile is to be installed over concrete, the surface must be smooth, level, and free from dirt, grease, old finishes and sealers, and other foreign matter. More importantly, the concrete floor must be perfectly dry when you install the tile and must not be subject to moisture penetration at any time. Moisture is a common problem with concrete floors poured directly on the ground ("on grade") and with concrete floors and walls that are below grade, as in a basement. Before you decide to install resilient tile on a concrete floor, you must test for moisture, preferably during a wet month. Test by taping some 1' square pieces of plastic to the floor, sealing all edges. After 24 hours lift them up; if there is moisture underneath, you should not put down resilient tile flooring. New concrete slabs should be allowed to cure for at least a month before a moisture test is made.

If the floor is usable, remove all foreign matter—paint, sealers, oil, grease, and so on. Clean oil and grease with a chemical garage floor cleaner, available from most auto supply stores. Chip or scrape off any excess concrete, paint, or other foreign material. To remove paint or sealers, sand the floor to bare concrete with a floor sander and #4 or #5 open-cut sandpaper. Remove high spots by rubbing with a coarse abrasive stone. Finish the preparation by scouring the floor with a stiff bristle brush and vacuuming up all loose material.

As a final step, fill cracks, joints, and low areas in the concrete with a concrete patching material. If the floor is too rough or uneven to be smoothed by the method given above, consider installing a plywood subfloor on sleepers or pouring a new slab over the old one.

Laying Resilient Floor Tile

When you lay resilient tile, the temperature is important. All materials should be unpacked and stacked for 24 hours in the room to be covered so floor and tile will be about the same in temperature and humidity. Room temperature should preferably be 65° or warmer for the 24 hours before and after installation.

Laying resilient tiles involves three basic operations: marking the working lines, spreading the adhesive (unless you're using self-stick tiles), and placing the tiles. For each operation carefully follow the step-by-step procedures outlined below, in conjunction with any instructions that come with the tile you're using.

Marking the working lines. The drawings below show how to mark working lines for square and diagonal tile patterns.

For a square pattern: Measure and mark the center points of the two longest opposite walls. Disregard any offsets, alcoves, or other breaks in the walls. Use a chalk line (available at most hardware stores) to snap a line between the two points for the first center line. Follow the same procedure for the other two walls, but check the intersection of the two lines with a carpenter's square before you snap the second line to make sure it is 90°. If it isn't, check both your measurements again.

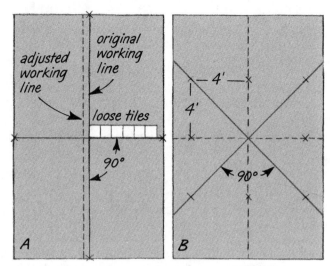

Working lines *for square tile pattern (A) and diagonal tile pattern (B) must intersect at exactly 90°.*

If the walls are out of line, use the square to adjust the second line until it is square with the first.

Next, lay a row of loose tiles along one of the lines from the center point to the wall. If the space between the last tile and the wall is less than one-half tile, move the center point one-half tile closer to the opposite wall and snap a new chalk line. Repeat this process with the other line. Doing this will ensure that the border tiles around the perimeter of the room are about equal in size and not too narrow.

For a diagonal pattern: Establish center lines as you would for the square pattern, making sure they intersect at right angles. Next, mark each line at a point 4' from the center. From these points, measure out 4' in each direction perpendicular to the center lines and mark points where these lines intersect, as shown in the drawing. Snap chalk lines across these points to get diagonal working lines. If your measurements are accurate, the diagonal lines will intersect at 90° exactly at the center point. If they don't, check your measurements.

Spreading the adhesive. Before you spread adhesive, be sure to read the instructions on the container label thoroughly. Most adhesives are troweled on, but some are rolled or brushed on. The proper trowel size is given on the label. The instructions will also tell you the open time—the amount of time you have to work with the adhesive. Spread the adhesive firmly with the notched trowel, which will ensure spreading the proper thickness.

Following application instructions on the label, begin spreading the adhesive near where the working lines intersect. Spread the adhesive up to, but not over, the working lines that will guide your tile placement. Be careful not to cover too large an area at one time, or the adhesive may set up before you can cover it; start with an area about 3' square.

Placing the tiles. Two methods for laying out a square tile pattern are shown at right. You can use either one,

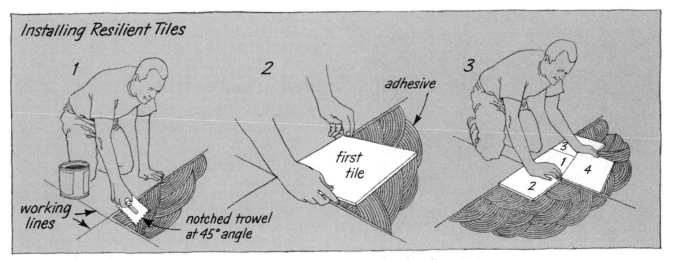

Installing Resilient Tiles

adhesive

first tile

working lines

notched trowel at 45° angle

To lay tiles: *(1) Spread adhesive evenly. (2) Align first tile in intersection of working lines. (3) Lay rest of tiles; match corners exactly.*

although it's best to use the method specified in the instructions that come with your tile. Method A is preferable when the open time of the adhesive allows you to cover a large area at a time.

Install the first tile in one of the right angles formed by the center lines. It's important that the first run of tiles be laid very carefully along the chalk lines. Fit the subsequent tiles with equal care to keep the lines straight. Continue laying the tiles in pyramid fashion to according to method A or method B. Place each tile tightly against adjacent tiles by touching the edges and then lowering the tile into place. Never slide tile into position or the adhesive will come up through the joints.

Once the tile is in position, press it firmly in place. Lay half a dozen or so; set them by going over them with a rolling pin.

If you're using self-stick tiles, take extra care to position them exactly before you press them into place. They're hard to remove once they are fixed to the floor. Also note the arrows on the back of self-stick tiles. The tiles should be laid with all the arrows going the same way.

When laying tile, work on the subfloor as long as possible. You'll have to move onto the tiles when you lay the tiles along the wall, after all the full tiles are down. Use plywood kneeling boards, about 3' square, under your knees and toes to distribute your weight on the tiles and to keep them from slipping. Move the boards carefully. Rubber knee pads, available for a few dollars at most hardware stores, will make the job more comfortable.

For a diagonal pattern, lay out the tiles as shown in method C. The last row of tiles you lay before installing border tiles will be diagonal half tiles. If you're using tiles of contrasting colors, (see the drawing on page 72), these half tiles should all be the same color.

If the tile has a pattern or grain running in one direction, cut either right or left half tiles to match the pattern or grain direction of the floor. Depending on how you cut the tile, you will end up with either two right or two left half tiles. If one wall requires left half tiles, then the opposite wall will also have left half tiles and the two adjacent walls will have right half tiles.

Cutting tile. In addition to cutting corner and border tiles, you may have to make irregular cuts in some of the tiles to fit around door jambs, pipes, or other obstacles in the room. To cut tiles, score along the mark with a utility knife and snap the tile along the line. For intricate cuts, use a pair of heavy scissors. The tiles will cut more easily in this case if warmed in sunlight or over a furnace vent. Don't overheat or the tiles may scorch or melt.

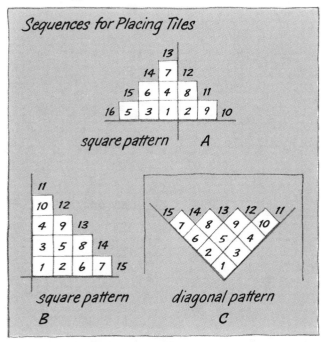

Sequences for Placing Tiles

square pattern   A

square pattern B

diagonal pattern C

Tiling sequences: *(A) half of floor at a time, (B) one-fourth of floor, (C) one-fourth of floor for diagonal pattern.*

right half tiles

left half tiles

cutting left
half tile

cutting right
half tile

Cutting and placing diagonal half tiles.

To mark and cut border tiles, position a loose tile exactly over one of the tiles in the last row closest to the wall (A) making sure that the grain or pattern is running in the right direction. Place another loose tile on top of the first, butting it against the wall (B). Using this tile as a guide, mark tile A with a pencil or score it with a utility knife. When cut, tile A will fit exactly in the border. Follow the same basic procedure for cutting corner tiles, as shown in the drawing below. You'll end up with an L-shaped tile.

For irregular areas, such as around a door jamb, use a contour gauge and transfer the outline to the tile. You can also cut a cardboard pattern to fit the space and trace the pattern onto a tile.

Finishing touches. Once you have laid all the tiles, make a final inspection to see that they are smooth, tight, and even. Be sure that no adhesive has seeped through the joints. Remove excess adhesive from the floor surface with a rag moistened with a small amount

of alcohol or the recommended solvent. Avoid getting solvent in the tile joints; it will loosen the tile. Clean all tools immediately after use.

Installing Resilient Tiles on Walls

To dress up a wall you can use any type of resilient floor tile, wood tiles, or resilient tiles designed especially for walls.

Preparing wall surfaces. Wall surfaces must be prepared in the same general way as floors: they must be clean, dry, and smooth. First remove the base molding and all the cover plates for electrical switches and outlets. Rough surfaces must be sanded, filled and smoothed with the recommended patching material or trowel-on underlayment as specified by the tile manufacturer. Existing wallpaper or similar wall coverings must be removed and the subsurface primed with the recommended primer.

Walls that are below grade, and thus subject to moisture penetration, must first be waterproofed and then furred out and covered with a suitable backing material; your tile dealer can help you choose one. If you're using hardboard for backing, cement tiles to the unfinished side.

Marking the working lines. After you have prepared the wall surface and removed the base molding, check the floor along the wall to see if it is level. If it isn't, find and mark the lowest spot. Then measure up to a point ¼" less than the width of the base molding, as shown in the drawing below. From this new point, measure up the wall a distance equal to four tiles to establish the height of your horizontal working line. Establish a level line across the wall through this point.

Next, measure and mark the midpoint of your horizontal line. Using the level, draw the vertical working

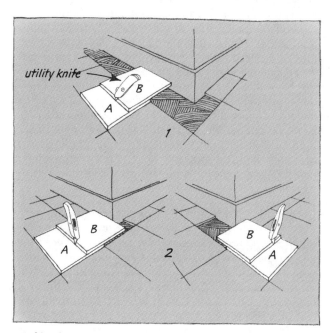

Marking border tiles: (1) against wall, (2) outside corner.

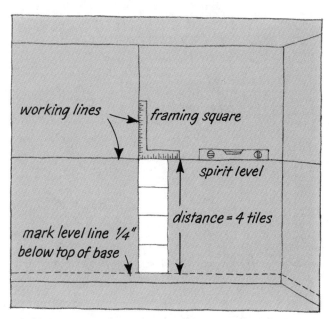

Establish working lines with level and framing square. Install tile up and down from horizontal line.

line through this point as shown in the illustration. With a square, check that the lines intersect at 90°.

The finished wall will look better if you avoid narrow border tiles at the corners of the walls. To arrange this, lay a row of loose tiles on the floor from the midpoint to the corner. If the space from the last full tile to the corner is less than one half tile, move the vertical working line over a distance of one half tile.

Installing the tiles. Use the correct adhesive for the wall surface, as specified by the tile manufacturer. Spread only enough adhesive to install 8 to 10 tiles at a time. When applying the tiles, follow one of the methods shown on page 71 for laying floor tiles. See the preceding instructions for cutting tiles. For a job with a finished look, you can install metal moldings and inside and outside metal corners. These and other types of molding are available where you buy resilient tiles.

Caring for Resilient Tile

High-quality vinyl tiles have a no-wax finish that generally requires only damp-mopping. Many manufacturers recommend that you refrain from washing a new floor for at least 3 days. This allows the adhesive to cure fully. During this time you can sweep the floor clean and remove spills with a damp cloth.

No-wax floors can benefit from special cleaners and finishes, especially after a few years of wear. Your dealer will carry products best suited to your particular floor.

To protect the floor from indentation, remove any small metal domes or glides from furniture legs, replacing them with wide glides or furniture cups like those shown in the drawing below. Replace hard, narrow rollers with wide, soft rubber casters.

Replacing Worn or Damaged Tiles

If your resilient floor is old enough that tiles have become worn in heavy traffic areas, you may have a hard time matching them. Even if you have some replacement tiles stashed away, new and old may differ

in color and thickness. If the worn tiles are confined to one area, such as that in front of a kitchen counter, you might be able to replace them by creating a design using a complementary pattern or color. Usually, though, you're better off replacing your old floor with new, longer-lasting tiles.

With today's resilient tile floors, wear is a less frequent cause for repair than is damage—cuts, cigarette burns, furniture marks, and so on. You'll probably have to replace only a few tiles, and most likely you'll have replacements or be able to find them.

To replace a damaged tile, first warm it and the adhesive below with a propane torch or an old iron. Pry up the tile using a putty knife or cold chisel. Remove any excess backing or adhesive from the floor until the surface is smooth and deep enough to install the new tile. Next, apply the proper adhesive, keeping it back about ¼" from the perimeter. Be careful not to get any on the surrounding tiles. Drop the new tile into place and press down firmly. Weights along the edges will ensure that the tile does not pop up before the adhesive sets.

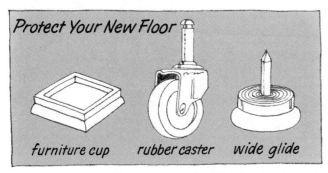

Floor protectors: *rubber casters, wide glides, furniture cups for heavy pieces.*

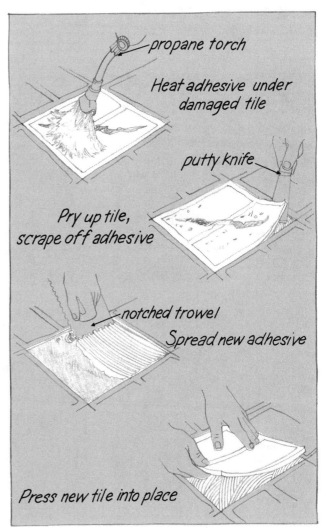

To replace a damaged tile, *follow the four steps illustrated above.*

Wood Tiles
. . . elegance with a touch of nature

Choose wood tiles *from a large assortment of styles, wood types, and finishes. Parquets shown here typify those available for do-it-yourself installation.*

Stone	**Haddon Hall**	**Fontainebleau**
Jeffersonian	**Canterbury**	**Finger Block**
Herringbone	**Parallel Finger Block**	**Louisville**

Floors of inlaid wood mosaic—known as parquet—once graced only the mansions of the elite. Today you can enjoy the warmth and elegance of these floors at a cost comparable to that of good-quality carpeting. And installing a parquet floor yourself can mean savings of more than half the cost of professional installation.

Parquet is made of wood tiles or wood blocks, and comes in a number of styles and patterns. Whether you choose a single style or create a combination, the warmth of wood will enhance the decor of your home with an esthetic statement of timeless elegance.

Visual appeal isn't the only reason for considering parquet. Modern factory-applied finishes are so tough and durable that they may outlast the mortgage. Even if heavy traffic wears through the finish, you can refinish the floor for a fraction of the cost of replacing other flooring materials. Wood is warm, perhaps second only to carpeting for warmth under bare feet. And the actual laying of a parquet floor is as easy as putting down a resilient tile floor.

Parquet need not be limited to floors. Applied to walls, it can add striking accents to a room. You can refurbish an old door with wood tiles to match the floor or rejuvenate an old table by covering it with parquet.

Choosing & Buying Parquet

Manufacturers produce scores of different parquet patterns; some of the more popular ones are illustrated on the facing page. Not all patterns are available from every retailer, so you may have to shop around to find a pattern you like. In addition, you have your choice among a variety of woods and textures, in both prefinished and unfinished tiles made of solid or laminated wood.

Types of Woods & Finishes

Wood tiles are made from many common and exotic hardwoods. You can have a parquet floor of red oak, white oak, maple, ash, walnut, pecan, or teak. Your choice will depend on personal taste, what is available, and cost. Cost is influenced by the type of wood, the intricacy of the pattern, and whether the tiles are prefinished or not.

Wood tiles come in two basic forms: solid wood or pieces of hardwood veneer laminated to plywood backing. Both types are available with either square or tongue-and-groove edges, depending on the pattern, thickness, and manufacturer. Both come prefinished, and the solid wood ones are also available unfinished.

Solid wood tiles. Solid wood tiles are made up of many small pieces of hardwood. They're a higher quality flooring material than the laminated tiles. The tiles range in size from 4" square to 16" square, with thicknesses from the fairly standard $5/16$" up to $3/4$" thick, but they may look small when installed. They are commonly mounted on a mesh backing, which allows you to put down 1 or 2 square feet at a time into the adhesive. Some tiles, however, are put down by nailing through the tongues.

Laminated wood tiles. Most laminated wood tiles are made of a thin layer of hardwood pieces glued to a plywood backing. A better quality of laminated wood tile has two layers of hardwood veneer, with the grain of one running perpendicular to the other for greater strength. Many of these prefinished wood tiles are also precut so you can readily separate an individual tile into smaller pieces that can fit easily along walls or be made into an intricate border pattern.

Prefinished wood tiles. The stain and protective coating on prefinished tiles are applied at the factory. The factory finish usually consists of a penetrating sealer baked into the wood with a urethane surface coat for easy maintenance. Putting down the prefinished tiles is a simple job.

Unfinished wood tiles. Used by most professional floorlayers, unfinished tiles are less expensive than the prefinished kind but require more work after they're laid. They will need sanding, staining, and one or more protective finish coats, and any cracks will need to be filled. But doing your own work can result in substantial savings and a finished floor markedly more attractive than prefinished parquet. You have a wide choice of wood, numerous patterns are available, and you can select from more colors if you do your own staining.

It's worth noting that putting down unfinished tiles and then doing all the finishing of the floor is a major undertaking. The house will be disrupted for several days and doorways will need to be covered with plastic sheeting to keep sanding particles from blowing into other rooms.

Surface texture. Although smooth parquet floors are frequently a favored choice, some manufacturers offer parquet made from uneven wood blocks, which give a more rustic or informal feeling. Once in place these are sanded until nearly smooth; there's nothing to trip over. These are often less expensive than the more carefully finished tiles.

Buying What You Need

First calculate the floor area by multiplying the length by the width of the room (in feet). If the room is irregular in shape, divide it into sections, find the area of each section, and add them together. Add 5 percent to the total so you'll have enough to cover cutting waste and mistakes and some leftovers to replace any damaged tiles. You can also use them for decorative purposes around the house, such as covering a table or countertop.

Depending on the size and type of wood tile you buy, a box will cover from 25 to 55 square feet. If the dealer stocks the pattern you choose, you can probably break a box and buy the exact number of tiles required. Should you have to order the tiles specially from a distributor, you may have to purchase full boxes.

The dealer will recommend the best type of adhesive and how much will be needed for the tile you buy. The adhesive is normally a mastic but can be an epoxy.

Tools You'll Need

Most of the tools you'll need are fairly common: steel measuring tape, hammer, putty knife, square, rubber mallet, chalk line, and saber saw or coping saw for cutting irregular outlines. A pair of rubber knee pads will make your work more comfortable.

You'll also need a notched trowel. The label on the adhesive usually states what size notches to use. The standard is a trowel with ½"-wide teeth and notches that are ¼" deep and ³⁄₁₆" wide.

Wood tiles need to be firmly bedded in the adhesive with a weighted floor roller, which can be rented. If you're putting down an unfinished parquet floor, you'll also have to rent a power floor sander to smooth the floor after it's laid. Power edgers for working next to the wall are available; you can also use a belt sander. If you haven't used a floor sander, practice on a full sheet of old plywood first because it takes a little practice to learn how to control one. Never let the sander remain in one spot while in use or it will immediately sand a depression in your floor.

How to Install Parquet

Laying a parquet floor, like laying any tile floor, requires careful attention to layout. If the working lines are accurate and the initial tiles are laid properly, it then becomes just a matter of laying one tile after another.

Preparation

You can put parquet down over a wide variety of surfaces, whether old or new, if they are firm, clean, smooth, and dry. Note that moisture is a real problem for parquet floors because the wood will swell when damp and start breaking loose. If your house is built with a crawlspace, rather than a dry basement or slab, cover the ground under the floor with plastic sheeting. Use stones to weight the edges so all ground moisture is trapped under the plastic and does not come up through the subfloor. Also, don't put parquet down on a surface that is below ground level because of the moisture problem.

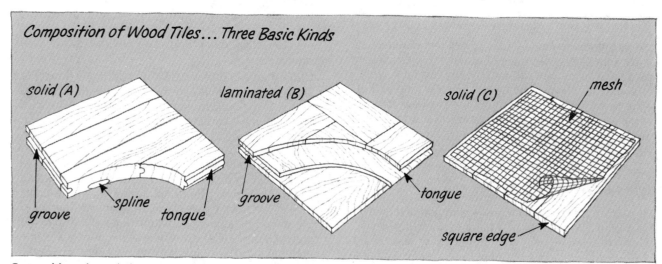

Composition of Wood Tiles... Three Basic Kinds

solid (A)   laminated (B)   solid (C)   mesh

groove   spline   tongue   groove   tongue   square edge

Composition *of wood tiles varies: solid (A and C) and laminated (B). Both come with either tongue-and-groove or square edges. Splines or mesh fasten hardwood pieces to form solid wood tiles; layers of wood are glued in laminated construction.*

Plywood surfaces. Ideally, subfloors should be 1¼" tongue-and-groove plywood, but if necessary you can use a minimum of ¾" plywood on joists spaced 16" on center (from the center of one joist to the center of the next one).

Use a straightedge rule to check that the floor is level within ¼" over 10 feet. Use a power floor sander to smooth all irregularities, and then fill any dips with an epoxy-base adhesive (see page 70) and let dry. If a wood floor is smooth but covered with shellac, varnish, or wax, sand the surface to roughen it for the adhesive.

Resilient tile surfaces. Parquet can be put over linoleum or vinyl tile floors if they are smooth and in good shape. If the vinyl tile is several years old, it may be vinyl-asbestos. In this case do not disturb it because the asbestos particles are a health hazard. If it is in good shape and not crumbly, clean it thoroughly to remove any wax and then put the wood tiles right over it. If the tile is in poor condition, cover it with ¼" plywood and then put down the wood tiles.

Concrete surfaces. Concrete makes a good subfloor if it is dry. To make sure, place 1' squares of plastic in half a dozen spots around the floor, carefully taping down all edges. This is best done during wet months. After 24 hours take up the plastic. If there is condensation underneath, moisture is coming through the concrete and it is unsuitable for parquet. If the concrete floor is dry, use a garage floor cleaner available at auto parts stores to remove grease and oil. Use a cold chisel to remove any chunks of concrete and fill depressions with a concrete patching mix.

Clearance. After the subfloor is clean and level, remove any baseboard and shoe molding. If you're laying the wood tiles over an existing floor, place a tile next to the door and mark where it needs to be cut to clear the new floor. Allow ¼" additional clearance for interior doors; on exterior doors allow for the type of weather-stripping used. Remove the doorway threshold. The door casings must be notched to permit the tile to slip underneath. Place a parquet tile next to the casing, mark and add ¼" for expansion, and then cut with a handsaw.

Marking the Working Lines

Once the subfloor is ready, mark the working lines. These are designed to keep the tile joints straight, even if your walls are not, and to ensure that the tiles cut along the walls are large enough to be visually appealing.

Begin by measuring to find the exact center of two facing walls, A and B. Snap a chalk line (AA) between the two center points. Find the center of walls C and D and again snap the chalk line (BB). To check that these lines cross at a 90° angle, meaning they are square, use the 3-4-5 method: From the center measure 3' down line AA and 4' down line BB. The diagonal distance between these two points will be exactly 5' if the lines are square. If not—and your measurements are correct—the walls are out of square. Adjust line BB until the diagonal is 5'.

Next, determine how the tiles are going to look around the borders. If they are about a half tile or larger in size they won't appear to be afterthoughts. Make a dry run with the parquet tiles down from the center along lines AA and BB. If the last piece is less than half a tile, move the center line a half tile to one side.

Spreading the Adhesive

The adhesive, like the tiles, should be left at room temperature for 24 hours to warm up. You can also put the can of adhesive in hot water to soften it. If the adhesive is still stiff, use a putty knife or piece of shingle to put it on the floor. Spread the adhesive with the notched trowel held at about a 30° angle. Work the adhesive from several different directions to spread it evenly. If you can't see the working lines through the adhesive, be careful not to cover them. Spread only as much as you can comfortably reach and can cover before it starts to dry.

Placing the Parquet

Place the first tile precisely along the intersecting lines. Take care to do this accurately because all remaining tiles will follow this one. Lay the second tile on the other side of the line, as illustrated, and then place the third and fourth tiles as shown. See that they're on the working lines and that they're butted together. Do not slide except for the small amount necessary with tongue-and-groove pieces.

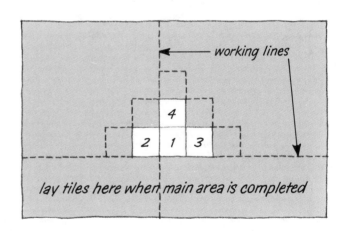

Continue laying the tile in pyramid fashion, working backward to stay off the tiles as long as possible. When you must get on the flooring, use two pieces of plywood about 2' square under your knees and toes to distribute your weight.

When cutting the pieces to fit along the wall, as illustrated on page 78, cut the tile ½" short of the wall. This permits the flooring to expand. If it can't, it may buckle. This gap will be covered by the baseboard or shoe molding.

(Continued on page 79)

Installing Wood Tiles . . . Step by Step

Step 1. *Spread adhesive with notched trowel. Do not cover working lines.*

Step 2. *Lay first tile. Align edges carefully with intersection of working lines.*

Step 3. *Place next three tiles. Match corners exactly; butt edges together tightly.*

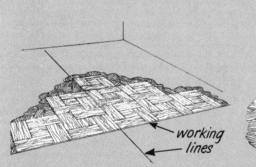

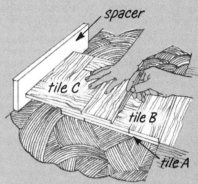

Step 4. *Install tiles across room, maintaining step pattern and tile alignment.*

Step 5. *Tap tiles with rubber mallet as you work to bed them and to lower any high corners.*

Step 6. *Set tile B for border exactly atop last full tile A. Set tile C against spacer; mark cutting line on tile B.*

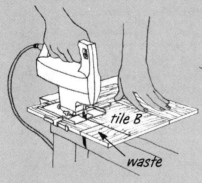

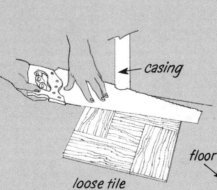

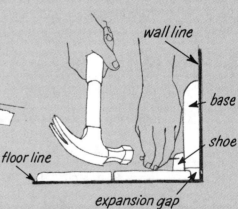

Step 7. *Use contour gauge to transfer irregular outlines, such as rock fireplace hearth, to tiles.*

Step 8. *Use saber saw to cut tiles. Place cut side next to wall.*

Step 9. *Leave ½" expansion gap between border tiles and wall. Nail molding or shoe molding to wall, not flooring, so tiles can expand toward walls.*

. . . Continued from page 77

Work to finish half a room at a time, but keep your eye on the clock. Within 4 hours of the time the tile was laid, you must roll it to set the tile fully and to level any pieces that have popped up. If you've rented the kind of weighted floor roller you fill with water, it should weigh about 150 pounds. Check that the surface of the roller is smooth and clean.

The outer edges of wood tiles in an exterior doorway should be carefully sealed before the threshold is replaced, to minimize water penetration.

If there is a difference in height between two interior floors, use a reducer strip—usually a matching piece of wood 1½" wide with a rounded nosing on the outer edge for a finished look.

Finishing the Floor

Finishing a parquet floor is fairly complicated. Here are a few hints; the *Sunset* book *Flooring* will give you full instructions.

Let the floor dry overnight and then sand the floor. Practice on some old plywood first if necessary; don't let the sander remain in one place or you'll damage the floor.

After sanding, vacuum the floor clean. Next, you apply a stain controller, which makes the stain go on evenly. Without it, different wood grains absorb the stain differently, often giving a blotchy appearance. The stain controller dries almost immediately and you can begin staining as soon as you're finished. Use rags to spread the stain and to control the degree of darkness—

the longer stain is allowed to stand before wiping, the darker it will be.

The floor can now be finished with urethane, which gives the appearance of permanent waxing without all the work. Urethane is usually brushed on and may take two coats. Ask your dealer for the recommended urethane. Or you can wax the floor.

Caring for the Floor

A good paste wax—not a water-based wax—will give added protection to the wood. Buff about twice a year; wax about once a year. Excessive waxing can cause wax to build up, detracting from the floor's appearance.

Dust-mop or vacuum your parquet floor as you would carpeting. Do not scrub or wet-mop the parquet. Use a damp cloth to remove fresh food spills.

Replacing a Tile

If you must replace a tile, first cut around the edges with a circular saw. Set the blade to the depth of the tile and don't damage adjoining tiles. Make some cross cuts in the middle and chisel the tile out. To make the new tile fit, first cut off the lower edge of the groove side. Now slip the tongue into the groove of an existing tile and press the new tile down.

GLOSSARY

Backing. 1) Any material used as a foundation for ceramic tile. 2) The underside of a resilient or wood tile.

Backsplash. The wall area covered with ceramic tile behind or around a sink or counter.

Base. 1) A flat wood molding used at the bottom of a wall to finish off a floor. Sometimes called base mold or molding. 2) *See* Backing, definition 1.

Batten. Wood strip usually 1" by 2" or 1" by 3".

Body. Structural portion of a ceramic tile as opposed to the finished top surface.

Bone pile. Stock of defective tiles and custom-order overruns maintained by some tile manufacturers; usually sold at a substantial discount.

Buttering. Spreading a thin coat of adhesive on the back of a tile just before placing it.

Chalk line. 1) String, coated with chalk, used to mark reference lines on a work surface. 2) The mark made on a working surface by snapping a stretched chalk line.

Culinarios. Traditional name for handpainted folk tiles.

Fume. To create an iridescent effect on ceramic tile by exposing the molten glaze to chemical fumes.

Furring. Wood strips used to build out a wall surface.

Glaze. Hard, glassy coating fused to the top surface of a ceramic tile by firing at a high temperature.

Grade. Ground level; floors are classified as above-grade, on-grade, or below-grade.

Handpainted. Decorative glaze applied to a ceramic tile by hand with a brush; hand-decorated.

Kickplate. Bottom of counter recessed for toe space.

Leg. Narrow column of ceramic tiles on the walls in front of a bathtub.

Mosaic. 1) Small ceramic tiles arranged in a pattern and joined into sheets by cotton or paper mesh or by dabs of silicone rubber. 2) Intricate pattern made with small ceramic tiles or pieces of ceramic tile, wood, glass, or stone.

Open time. Time during which an adhesive retains its ability to stick to a tile and bond it to a backing.

Parquet. 1) Floor made with an inlaid mosaic of wood. 2) A wood tile composed of several pieces of wood arranged in a pattern.

Receptor. Waterproof base for a shower.

Scraffito. A technique for decorating ceramic tile by cutting through the glaze before firing to expose the tile body.

Seconds. Tiles with minor defects of glaze, color, or form; usually sold at a substantial discount.

Sleepers. Lengths of lumber fastened to a concrete floor to support a wood subfloor.

Splines. Thin wood, metal, or plastic strips on the underside of a wood tile that hold the individual pieces of wood together.

Stoneware. Type of high-temperature-fired ceramic body with red spots of iron pulled to the surface by the temperature.

Terra cotta. 1) An inexpensive, low-temperature-fired ceramic tile. 2) A color, brownish orange.

Tesserae. Very small, square, individual ceramic tiles. *See also* Mosaic.

Trompe l'oeil. Decorated surface that creates an illusion of reality.

Underlayment. Material used to smooth and level irregularities in subfloors. Underlayments may be made of plywood, particle board (if made specifically for this purpose), hardboard, and several types of pliable coatings.

Wainscot. A facing such as ceramic, resilient, or wood tile applied to the lower part of a wall.

INDEX